PRÉVERSITIES

A Jacques Prévert Sampler

Norman R. Shapiro

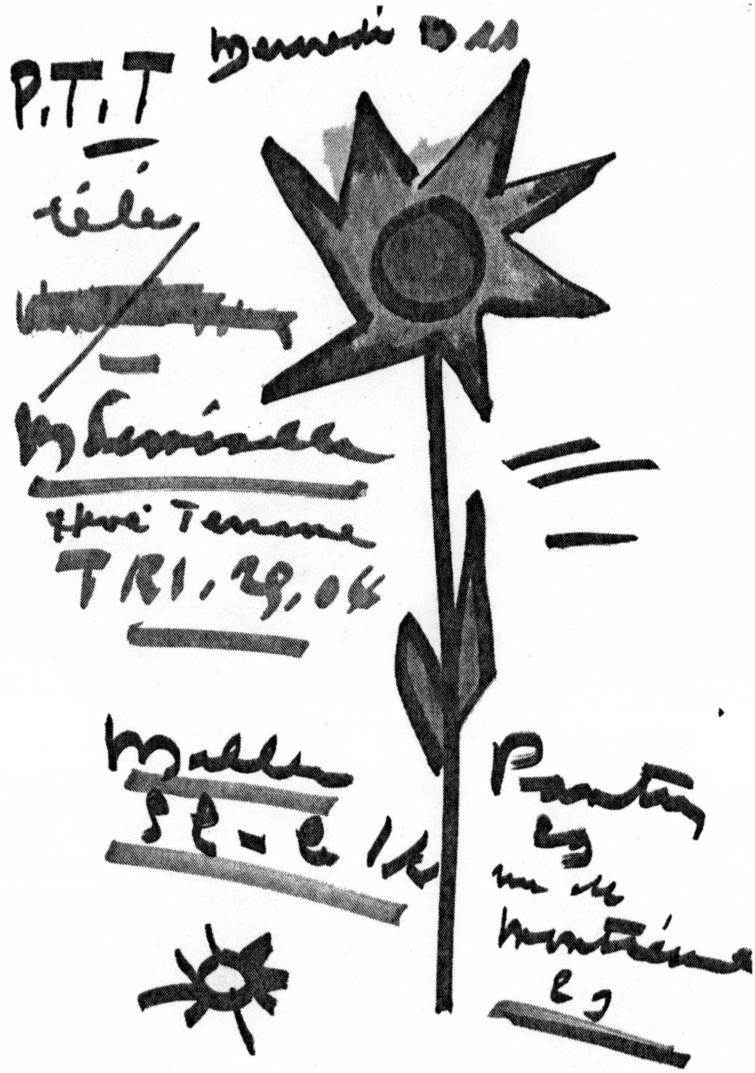
P.T.T

Préversities

A Jacques Prévert Sampler

Norman R. Shapiro

Introduction by Jeffrey Mehlman

BLACK WIDOW PRESS
BOSTON, MA

Préversities: A Jacques Prévert Sampler
English language translations © 2010 Norman R. Shapiro. Introduction ©
2010 Jeffrey Mehlman. Published by arrangement with Editions GALLI-
MARD, Paris. All Jacques Prévert's works contained within this edition © Edi-
tions GALLIMARD. Black Widow Press wishes to thank Wesleyan University
for its support. Publication of this book has been aided by a grant from the
Thomas and Catharine McMahon Fund of Wesleyan University, established
through the generosity of the late Joseph McMahon.

Black Widow Press is an imprint of Commonwealth Books, Inc., Boston, MA.
Distributed to the trade by NBN (National Book Network) throughout North
America, Canada, and the U.K. All Black Widow Press books are printed on acid-
free paper. Black Widow Press and its logo are registered trademarks of Common-
wealth Books, Inc.

Joseph S. Phillips and Susan J. Wood, PhD., Publishers
www.blackwidowpress.com

Book Design and Production: Kerrie Kemperman

Cover photo: Jacques Prévert, Rue du Chateau, ca. 1926.
    © Collection Catherine Prévert
Frontis: Ephemesis by Jacques Prévert © Fatras/Jacques Prévert Estate,
    Collection Jacques Prévert

ISBN-13: 978-0-9818088-2-6

Library of Congress Cataloging-in-Publication Data on file

10 9 8 7 6 5 4 3 2

Printed in the U.S.A.

To the happy memory

of two treasured friends,

Carl and Jane Viggiani

For the courtesy and consideration they have extended to me in the preparation of this collection, I am happy to thank Mmes Anne Remlinger, Eugénie Bachelot Prévert, and Catherine Prévert, of the Jacques Prévert Estate, as well as Mme Florence Giry of Gallimard et Cie., Paris.

My very special thanks go also to Jeffrey Mehlman, not only for his unique and graciously informative introduction, but also for having given me the opportunity to preview a number of these translations at Boston University as part of his Translation Seminar; to J. French Wall, for his invaluable help in coaxing me over a variety of electronic hurdles; and to Joseph Phillips of Black Widow Press, for his confidence in my work and his good humor in helping me bring it before the public.

It is always a pleasure to thank friends Evelyn Singer Simha and Caldwell Titcomb for their continuing and much appreciated encouragement.

TABLE OF CONTENTS

Photo booth montage
Jacques Prévert, circa 1930

INTRODUCTION

Jacques Prévert, the most popular French poet of the twentieth century, once observed that he had occasionally been inclined to put an end to his days, but could never decide which one to begin with. The line is a bravura exercise in what Norman Shapiro calls *preversity*. A statement depressive to the point of suicide is deepened, violated, "preverted" into an affirmation of life: "one's days" being interpreted no longer as "one's life" but as a series of discrete intervals, each too rich in experience to allow the poet to imagine it as anything other than endless. Small wonder, then, that Prévert, who once described himself—perversely—as "writing in bad French for bad Frenchmen," should emerge as a popular favorite: there are close to five hundred schools in France bearing the name of Jacques Prévert.

Reading through Norman Shapiro's rich anthology, which follows Prévert from the breakaway success of *Paroles* in 1945 to the posthumous *Soleil de nuit,* one is inclined to see in the end-of-days crack a kind of Prévertian proto-poem. Readers will recognize the gesture of the class dunce ("Le cancre") who, "with sticks of every color of chalk," manages to trace the face of happiness on the "damnable blackboard of distress." The configuration, duly transposed, will give us a poetics—in the Japanese water lily "of many a hue and shade," evolving from paper ball in straw to the subject of an awe that will never fade in the eyes of the children watching it blossom in water ("The School of Fine Arts"). But it will give us an erotics—in the "night-sky sun" of "Blood Orange"—and even a politics as well: a factory worker, upon seeing the sun suddenly smile "in his leaden sky," is prompted, in "Wasted Weather," to an act of rank insubordination…

That insubordination brings to mind Prévert's endearing anti-authoritarian streak, whose targets included the military, the family, school, and, most strikingly, religion. In the early 1970s, at a lunch at the home of the legendary psychoanalyst Jacques Lacan, I was treated to a recollection on the part of the actress Sylvie Bataille, Lacan's wife, relating to Prévert. She, Lacan, and Prévert, I was told, had managed—no small task!—to force their way into Notre-Dame for the mass celebrating the Liberation of Paris on August 26, 1944. Midway into the service, sniper-fire, the last stand of the dead-enders of Collaboration, was heard issuing from various recesses of the cathedral: Prévert immediately dived into a confessional, screaming that he didn't want to die in a church. With the exception of de Gaulle and Lacan (and this was the point of the story), every one else dived for cover amidst the pews.

For years it has seemed to me that the interest of the story lay with Lacan: in his identification with de Gaulle, or perhaps, more perversely, in just what he may have been doing during the war in order to be willing to risk his life in order to be seen standing with de Gaulle at war's end. Norman Shapiro's volume of translations opens up another facet of the story: Prévert's anti-clericalism, to be sure, but also just what the friendship between the famously abstruse psychoanalyst and the eminently readable poet may have been sustained by. The two were marginal members of the Surrealist group (with whom, Prévert said, he had "done his humanities"). But what strikes a reader of some of these poems is a theoretical richness no less profound than that found in some of the formulations of Lacan. There is the case of the two lovers (in "The Shadows"), ultimately less faithful to each other than their own shadows are to each of them, as faithful as a "brace of hounds" to their master or mistress, awaiting their death so they may gnaw on their bones. Has the triumph of Thanatos over Eros ever been couched more grippingly? Or consider "Picasso Out Strolling." A naïve painter, eager to depict an apple, comes to realize, in true paranoid fashion, that all the apple's "appearances are against him," whereupon a third instance surfaces in the poem: Picasso, who eats the apple, breaks the plate, and leaves the painter, "yanked out of his dreams like a tooth," alone "in the midst of his smashed crockery and the terrifying seeds of reality." Picasso indeed, but one is tempted to argue that Lacan, at his best, proceeded no differently with the conventions of psychoanalysis.

Unless, of course, Prévert managed to one-up Lacan himself. Consider the poet's version of the myth of Narcissus. The hero, aroused by the sight of a bevy of girls while he is swimming in the nude, emerges from the water, then retreats, perhaps embarrassed by his state of arousal, and, standing up to his waist in water, sees, "thanks to the phenomenon of refraction a shaft bending in two." Out of sheer despair, he drowns. A mirage of "castration" as the subtlest ruse of narcissism? It would take years for French psychoanalysis, in the person of Jean Laplanche, to supply that corrective to Lacanian dogma, but Prévert, in his poem, appears to be well ahead of the theorist's game.

The anecdote of Lacan and Prévert in Notre Dame merits mention as well for its relation to the career of Norman Shapiro. For whereas an entire generation of French scholars appears to have cast its academic lot with the intricacies of theorists such as Lacan and his distinguished ilk, Norman Shapiro has undertaken a far more solitary and original path: the recreation, as if from within, of French poetry in English.

The choice of Prévert, a major poet who is also a children's favorite, seems a natural for a translator who has given bravura versions of the entirety of La Fontaine's fables. In between there have been unforgettable volumes of Baudelaire, Verlaine, and many more. The pleasure of reading Norman Shapiro's translations, for this reader, is akin to the enjoyment of manipulating a kaleidoscope. All the fragments of the original manage to end up in the translation, but placed, economically and gracefully, differently. The poems themselves invariably please, but the relation between the original and the translation frequently dazzles. Which is to say that the reader of this dual-language volume is superlatively well-placed to intuit what André Breton may have meant when he said that Jacques Prévert was the only man he could not bear to see die.

—Jeffrey Mehlman

TRANSLATOR'S PREFACE

Americans who might think they know nothing at all about the quix-otic 20th-century French poet Jacques Prévert (1900–1977)—eminent wordsmith extraordinaire, with many varied strings to his stylistic bow—probably have met him from time to time without realizing it. Perhaps they have seen one or more of his screenplays—among them *Drôle de drame (Bizarre, Bizarre)* and *Quai des brumes (Port of Shadows)*—or enjoyed some of his popular song lyrics, in either French or English. Yves Mon-tand's performance of composer Joseph Kosma's melancholy favorite "Les Feuilles mortes" ("Autumn Leaves") is a likely example. Or maybe they were even exposed to some of his more rhetorically direct poems. The wartime "Barbara" or the pathetic "Déjeuner du matin" ("Morning Break-fast") come to mind, both favorites often used—thanks to their transparent grammar and simple vocabulary—in beginning or intermediate French classes.

It was for this simplicity of much of his verse, usually free rather than formal, with little strict rhyme or traditional French meter, that I assigned a number of Prévert's shorter texts, a few years ago, to my students in a workshop course in literary translation. The poems' seeming lack of com-plexity made them appear to be ideal pieces on which novices might cut their translators' teeth. To be sure, that "seeming lack of complexity" often proved to be just that—seeming—as we would all find out.

I chose first his uncomplicated but striking "Familiale," a good example of a poem with an easily understood message: an anti-war message found in much of his socio-political verse. And, as usual, when assigning a work, I thought it was only fair that I should attempt a translation myself. But the students and I would quickly discover that, for all its repetitive sim-plicity, the poem's subtleties of rhythm and sound begged to produce in English the same—or almost—effect of the original. Their results were varied, as one would expect. Some students captured bits and pieces: the informal, scattered rhymes, the incantatory quality of its repetitions, the scenario's monotonous and tragic despair. Others, alas, were doggedly inartistic, refusing to shake loose the bone of literal word-for-word equivalence from their eagerly clenched jaws.

My own version, in these pages, set me on the endeavor that, months later, was to become the present collection.

I had already read and reveled in as much of Prévert as most students and admirers of French poetry, but, with two exceptions, I had not attempted to translate him. Those exceptions had been "Le Chat et l'Oiseau" ("The Cat and the Bird") and "Chanson des escargots qui vont à l'enterrement" ("Song About the Snails Who Go Off to the Funeral"). The former, the only self-described "fable" in his oeuvre, was included in my collection *The Fabulists French: Verse Fables of Nine Centuries* (University of Illinois, 1992); the latter, sadly, was my contribution to a memorial service years ago for my dear colleague Susan Frazer, for whom the poem had always been a favorite. Armed then with three Prévert translations, I felt like the boat-builder who finds a ship's steering wheel and can't resist building the rest of the boat around it, lest it go to waste. The result is before you.

Even a casual leaf-through should reveal to the reader the variety, verve, and vitality that was—no, *is*—the poetic genius of Jacques Prévert. I have tried to illustrate those qualities in my selection, choosing the longish and the short, even the ultra-short; the unadornedly narrative and the dialogue-embellished dramatic; the quirkily rhymed and the straighforwardly prosy; the wryly serious and the punnishly droll, full of egregious wordplay that recalls Raymond Queneau and the surrealists. The reader will find many that exploit the vast, eternal themes of death, love—young love especially—and even more that paint Prévert's idiosyncratic everyday vignettes, tucked in among his more weighty concerns for society's foibles, war's stupidity, history's comic contradictions, religion's shortcomings, and man's self-important folly in many of its guises. And not without a dose of mild obscenity. A number are even aimed at children, young and adult…

All are offered here—preserving the originals' vagaries of format, punctuation, etc.—with the realization that the panorama presents only a fraction of Prévert's rich and varied poetic (and prose-poetic) repertory; but enough, I hope, to explain and excuse its lovingly outrageous title: *Préversities: A Jacques Prévert Sampler.*

—Norman R. Shapiro

PAROLES

(1945)

LA BELLE SAISON[1]

A jeun perdue glacée[2]
Toute seule sans un sou
Une fille de seize ans
Immobile debout
Place de la Concorde
A midi le Quinze Août.

THE FAIR WEATHER SEASON

Noon on fifteen August this
Paupered sixteen-year-old miss
Place de la Concorde
Frozen motionless
Hungry lost ignored
In summer loneliness.

---

[1] Given the very specific summer reference, *"la belle saison,"* usually synonymous with *"le printemps"* (spring) obviously shouldn't be taken literally.

[2] Likewise the adjective *"glacée"* (frozen).

ALICANTE

Une orange sur la table
Ta robe sur le tapis
Et toi dans mon lit
Doux présent du présent
Fraîcheur de la nuit
Chaleur de ma vie.

ALICANTE[1]

Orange on the table
Dress on the carpet round your feet
You lying in my bed
Gift of the present present sweet
Night cool and fresh
Heat of my flesh.

---

[1] Alicante is the capital city of the southeastern Spanish province of the same name, on the Mediterranean, known for its delightful climate, its Valencia oranges, and especially its foreign tourists. Prévert and actress Jacqueline Laurent were among the latter on a trip in 1936.

J'EN AI VU PLUSIEURS...

J'en ai vu un qui s'était assis sur le chapeau d'un autre
il était pâle
il tremblait
il attendait quelque chose... n'importe quoi...
la guerre... la fin du monde...
il lui était absolument impossible de faire un geste
ou de parler
et l'autre
l'autre qui cherchait « son » chapeau était plus pâle encore
et lui aussi tremblait
et se répétait sans cesse:
mon chapeau... mon chapeau...
et il avait envie de pleurer
J'en ai vu un qui lisait les journaux
j'en ai vu un qui saluait le drapeau
j'en ai vu un qui était habillé de noir
il avait une montre
une chaîne de montre
un porte-monnaie
la légion d'honneur
et un pince-nez.
J'en ai vu un qui tirait son enfant par la main
et qui criait...
j'en ai vu un avec un chien
j'en ai vu un avec une canne à épée
j'en ai vu un qui pleurait
j'en ai vu un qui entrait dans une église
j'en ai vu un autre qui en sortait...

I SAW THIS ONE AND THAT...

I saw one who had sat down on another man's hat
he was pale
he was trembling
he was waiting for something... anything at all...
war... the end of the world...
he was utterly unable to make the slightest move
or to speak
and the other one
the one who was looking for "his" hat was paler still
and he was trembling too
and saying to himself again and again
my hat... my hat...
and he felt like crying
I saw one reading the papers
I saw one saluting the flag
I saw one dressed in black
he had a watch
a watch-chain
a change-purse
the legion of honor
and a pince-nez
I saw one who was tugging his child by the hand
and who was yelling...
I saw one with a dog
I saw one with a sword-cane
I saw one who was in tears
I saw one who was going into a church
I saw another one who was leaving...

PATER NOSTER

Notre Père qui êtes aux cieux
Restez-y
Et nous nous resterons sur la terre
Qui est quelquefois si jolie
Avec ses mystères de New York
Et puis ses mystères de Paris
Qui valent bien celui de la Trinité
Avec son petit canal de l'Ourcq
Sa grande muraille de Chine
Sa rivière de Morlaix
Ses bêtises de Cambrai
Avec son océan Pacifique
Et ses deux bassins aux Tuileries
Avec ses bons enfants et ses mauvais sujets
Avec toutes les merveilles du monde
Qui sont là
Simplement sur la terre
Offertes à tout le monde
Éparpillées
Émerveillées elles-mêmes d'être de telles merveilles
Et qui n'osent se l'avouer
Comme une jolie fille nue qui n'ose se montrer
Avec les épouvantables malheurs du monde
Qui sont légion
Avec leurs légionnaires
Avec leurs tortionnaires
Avec les maîtres de ce monde

PATER NOSTER

Our father who art in heaven
Stay put
And we'll stay here on earth
That sometimes is so pretty
With its mysteries of New York City[1]
And its Paris mysteries
As good as the Trinity's
With its little canal at Ourcq
Its Great Wall of China
Its brook at Morlaix
Its candies from Cambrai
Its Pacific Ocean sea
And its two pools at the Tuileries
With its good kids and spoiled brats
With all its wonders of the world
Over the land
Offered free for the asking
Sprinkled liberally
Marvels marveling at their marvelousness
And basking in it all but not daring to confess
Their wonders to themselves
Like a beautiful nude who doesn't dare undress
With all the torturous horrors of the world
A veritable legion
With their legionaries[2]
With their mercenaries
Their sanguinaries

Les maîtres avec leurs prêtres leurs traîtres et leurs
reîtres
Avec les saisons
Avec les années
Avec les jolies filles et avec les vieux cons
Avec la paille de la misère pourrissant dans l'acier des
canons.

With the masters of this world
The masters with their pastors their traitors collaborators
With the seasons
With the years
With young girls and doddering old men assholes
With rotting straw wadding in cannon-barrel-brass[3] holes.

---

[1] The allusions to New York and Paris "mysteries" are specific. The first refers to the French title of an American silent film serial, *Les Mystères de New-York*, from around 1915, by French director Louis Gasnier, starring Pearl White, of *Perils of Pauline* fame; the second, to a novel, *Les Mystères de Paris*, by Eugène Sue, published first as a weekly serial from 1842 to 1843 with phenomenal success.

[2] In reproducing Prévert's meaning here, without slavishly following him line for line, I think my turning "sanguinary" into a noun isn't too far from his own typical liberties.

[3] My interpretation of *"paille"* here may differ from others'. Also, since cannon barrels were, in fact, usually made of bronze—not Prévert's *"acier"* (steel)—I settle on brass for obvious and, I hope, excusable reasons.

LE CANCRE

Il dit non avec la tête
mais il dit oui avec le cœur
il dit oui à ce qu'il aime
il dit non au professeur
il est debout
on le questionne
et tous les problèmes sont posés
soudain le fou rire le prend
et il efface tout
les chiffres et les mots
les dates et les noms
les phrases et les pièges
et malgré les menaces du maître
sous les huées des enfants prodiges
avec des craies de toutes les couleurs
sur le tableau noir du malheur
il dessine le visage du bonheur.

THE DUNCE

He says no with his head
with his heart he says just so
he says just so to what he loves
to the teacher he says no
he's standing there
he's being questioned
and all the problems have been asked
suddenly he bursts out in a giggle
and he wipes the board bare
the figures the words
the dates the names
the sentences the traps and tricks
and despite the master's threatened raps
as the prodigy children hiss and squawk
with sticks of every color of chalk
over the blackboard of sad distress
he sketches the face of happiness.

CHANSON DES ESCARGOTS
QUI VONT À L'ENTERREMENT

À l'enterrement d'une feuille morte
Deux escargots s'en vont
Ils ont la coquille noire
Du crêpe autour des cornes
Ils s'en vont dans le soir
Un très beau soir d'automne
Hélas quand ils arrivent
C'est déjà le printemps
Les feuilles qui étaient mortes
Sont toutes ressuscitées
Et les deux escargots
Sont très désappointés
Mais voilà le soleil
Le soleil qui leur dit
Prenez prenez la peine
La peine de vous asseoir
Prenez un verre de bière
Si le cœur vous en dit
Prenez si ça vous plaît
L'autocar pour Paris
Il partira ce soir
Vous verrez du pays
Mais ne prenez pas le deuil
C'est moi qui vous le dis
Ça noircit le blanc de l'œil
Et puis ça enlaidit
Les histoires de cercueils
C'est triste et pas joli
Reprenez vos couleurs
Les couleurs de la vie

SONG ABOUT THE SNAILS
WHO GO OFF TO THE FUNERAL

Off to a dead leaf's funeral
There go a pair of snails
The shells they wear are black
With crepe around their horns
Off in the dark they go
One lovely autumn night
But when they get there   Oh
Already spring has come
And all the fall's dead leaves
Have sprung to life again
And so our pair of snails
Feel very low   But then
But then and there the sun
The sun he says   Here here
Come take a seat you two
And have yourselves a beer
A beer if that's your pleasure
Or if you'd rather take
A trip to gay Paree
The bus it leaves tonight
Many a sight you'll see
So take your pick   Just leave
Your mourning-clothes behind
I'm telling you   I know
They'll turn your eyeballs black
Besides it's much too sad
This graveyard talk and such
It makes you look so bad
So take your colors back
The colors of living life

Alors toutes les bêtes
Les arbres et les plantes
Se mettent à chanter
À chanter à tue-tête
La vraie chanson vivante
La chanson de l'été
Et tout le monde de boire
Tout le monde de trinquer
C'est un très joli soir
Un joli soir d'été
Et les deux escargots
S'en retournent chez eux
Ils s'en vont très émus
Ils s'en vont très heureux
Comme ils ont beaucoup bu
Ils titubent un p'tit peu
Mais là-haut dans le ciel
La lune veille sur eux.

Then all the beasts the trees
The plants they start to sing
To sing their heads off singing
The living song of summer
And everyone begins
To drink and clink their cups
That very lovely night
That lovely summer night
And so our snails go home
They go with happy hearts
They go with spirits high
And since they've drunk a lot
They stagger just a bit
But up there in the sky
The moon looks down on them
And keeps a watchful eye.

FAMILIALE

La mère fait du tricot
Le fils fait la guerre
Elle trouve ça tout naturel la mère
Et le père qu'est-ce qu'il fait le père?
Il fait des affaires
Sa femme fait du tricot
Son fils la guerre
Lui des affaires
Il trouve ça tout naturel le père
Et le fils et le fils
Qu'est-ce qu'il trouve le fils?
Il ne trouve rien absolument rien le fils
Le fils sa mère fait du tricot son père des affaires lui la guerre
Quand il aura fini la guerre
Il fera des affaires avec son père
La guerre continue la mère continue elle tricote
Le père continue il fait des affaires
Le fils est tué il ne continue plus
Le père et la mère vont au cimetière
Ils trouvent ça tout naturel le père et la mère
La vie continue la vie avec le tricot la guerre les affaires
Les affaires la guerre le tricot la guerre
Les affaires les affaires et les affaires
La vie avec le cimetière.

FAMILY SCENE

Mammá's at her knitting
The son's at his war
No need to ask herself what for
It's only fitting thinks mammá
And papá what's he at what's he at papá?
Papá's at his business good bourgeois
His wife's at her knitting
His son's at his war
And he's at his business nothing more
No need to ask himself what for
It's only fitting thinks papá
And son thinks what does son think... Think? Bah!
Son doesn't think... Mammá's at her knitting
Papá's at his business son's at his war et cetera et cetera
And when his war's done
He'll go into business with papá
But war keeps on mammá keeps at her knitting
Papá keeps at his business like before
The son gets killed does nothing more
Papá mammá go graveyard-sitting
No need to ask themselves what for?
It's only proper only fitting
And life keeps on life with its war life with its knitting
Business and knitting business and war
Business and business little more
Business and life and graveyard-sitting.

PAGE D'ÉCRITURE

Deux et deux quatre
quatre et quatre huit
huit et huit font seize...
Répétez! dit le maître
Deux et deux quatre
quatre et quatre huit
huit et huit font seize.
Mais voilà l'oiseau-lyre
qui passe dans le ciel
l'enfant le voit
l'enfant l'entend
l'enfant l'appelle:
Sauve-moi
joue avec moi
oiseau!
Alors l'oiseau descend
et joue avec l'enfant
Deux et deux quatre...
Répétez! dit le maître
et l'enfant joue
l'oiseau joue avec lui...
Quatre et quatre huit
huit et huit font seize
et seize et seize qu'est-ce qu'ils font?
Ils ne font rien seize et seize
et surtout pas trente-deux
de toute façon
et ils s'en vont.
Et l'enfant a caché l'oiseau
dans son pupitre
et tous les enfants

SCRIPT

Two and two four
four and four eight
eight and eight make sixteen...
Again! says the teacher
Two and two four
four and four eight
eight and eight make sixteen
But suddenly the lyre-bird
flies by in the sky
the child sees it
the child hears it
the child calls to it
Save me
play with me
bird!
So the bird flies down
and plays with the child
Two and two four...
Again! says the teacher
and the child is playing
the bird is playing with him...
Four and four eight
eight and eight make sixteen
and sixteen and sixteen what do they make?
They make nothing at all sixteen and sixteen
and certainly not thirty-two
at any rate
and they go running off
And the child has hidden the bird
in his desk
and all the children

entendent sa chanson
et tous les enfants
entendent la musique
et huit et huit à leur tour s'en vont
et quatre et quatre et deux et deux
à leur tour fichent le camp
et un et un ne font ni une ni deux
un à un s'en vont également.
Et l'oiseau-lyre joue
et l'enfant chante
et le professeur crie:
Quand vous aurez fini de faire le pitre!
Mais tous les autres enfants
écoutent la musique
et les murs de la classe
s'écroulent tranquillement.
Et les vitres redeviennent sable
l'encre redevient eau
les pupitres redeviennent arbres
la craie redevient falaise
le porte-plume redevient oiseau.

can hear its song
and all the children
can hear the music
and eight and eight go running off next
and four and four and two and two
tell it all to go screw
and go running off next
and one and one don't make either one or two
one and one go running off as well
And the lyre-bird keeps playing
and the child keeps singing
and the teacher keeps yelling:
When are you going to stop being a clown!
But all the other children
are listening to the music
and the schoolroom walls
come quietly crumbling
tumbling down
and the window panes turn back to sand
the ink turns back to water
the desks turn back to trees
the chalk turns back to cliffs
the quill-pen turns back to bird.

POUR FAIRE LE PORTRAIT
D'UN OISEAU

À Elsa Henriquez

Peindre d'abord une cage
avec une porte ouverte
peindre ensuite
quelque chose de joli
quelque chose de simple
quelque chose de beau
quelque chose d'utile
pour l'oiseau
placer ensuite la toile contre un arbre
dans un jardin
dans un bois
ou dans une forêt
se cacher derrière l'arbre
sans rien dire
sans bouger...
Parfois l'oiseau arrive vite
mais il peut aussi bien mettre de longues années
avant de se décider
Ne pas se décourager
attendre
attendre s'il le faut pendant des années
la vitesse ou la lenteur de l'arrivée
de l'oiseau n'ayant aucun rapport
avec la réussite du tableau
Quand l'oiseau arrive
s'il arrive
observer le plus profond silence
attendre que l'oiseau entre dans la cage

HOW TO PAINT THE PORTRAIT
OF A BIRD

For Elsa Henriquez[1]

First paint a cage
with an open door
next paint
something nice
something simple
something pretty
something useful
for the bird
next place the canvas against a tree
in a garden
in a wood
or in a forest
go hide behind the tree
and keep very silent
and keep very still...
Sometimes the bird will come right away
but it also might take it years and years
to make up its mind
Don't get discouraged
wait
wait for years if you have to
since the speed or the delay of the bird's approach
has nothing to do
with the portrait's success
When the bird arrives
if it arrives
observe absolute silence
wait for the bird to go into the cage

et quand il est entré
fermer doucement la porte avec le pinceau
puis
effacer un à un tous les barreaux
en ayant soin de ne toucher aucune des plumes de l'oiseau
Faire ensuite le portrait de l'arbre
en choisissant la plus belle de ses branches
pour l'oiseau
peindre aussi le vert feuillage et la fraîcheur du vent
la poussière du soleil
et le bruit des bêtes de l'herbe dans la chaleur de l'été
et puis attendre que l'oiseau se décide à chanter
Si l'oiseau ne chante pas
c'est mauvais signe
signe que le tableau est mauvais
mais s'il chante c'est bon signe
signe que vous pouvez signer
alors vous arrachez tout doucement
une des plumes de l'oiseau
et vous écrivez votre nom dans un coin du tableau.

and when it is inside
close the door with the brush
then
rub out all the bars one by one
careful not to touch a single one of the bird's feathers
Next paint the picture of the tree
choosing the prettiest one of its branches
for the bird
paint the greenery too and the cool breeze as well
the dust in the sunlight
and the chirping of the insects in the grass in summer's heat
and then wait for the bird to make up its mind to sing
If the bird doesn't sing
that will be a bad sign
a sign that the portrait is bad
but if it sings it's a good sign
a sign that you may sign it
so gently as you can you pluck
one of the bird's feathers
and you sign your name in a corner of the canvas.

---

[1] Elsa Henriquez, well-known book illustrator, did the illustrations for Prévert's
children's collection, *Contes pour enfants pas sages* (Paris: Le Pré aux Clercs, 1947).

SABLES MOUVANTS

Démons et merveilles
Vents et marées
Au loin déjà la mer s'est retirée
Et toi
Comme une algue doucement caressée par le vent
Dans les sables du lit tu remues en rêvant
Démons et merveilles
Vents et marées
Au loin déjà la mer s'est retirée
Mais dans tes yeux entr'ouverts
Deux petites vagues sont restées
Démons et merveilles
Vents et marées
Deux petites vagues pour me noyer.

QUICKSAND

Demons and wonders
Wind and tide
The waters have receded far and wide
And you
Like seaweed with the soft breeze ſtroking her
Dreaming amid the bed of sand you ſtir
Demons and wonders
Wind and tide
The waters have receded far and wide
But in your eyes dim-lidded two
Little waves have remained where they had been
Demons and wonders
Wind and tide
Two little waves to drown me in.

LE DROIT CHEMIN

À chaque kilomètre
chaque année
des vieillards au front borné
indiquent aux enfants la route
d'un geste de ciment armé.

THE PROPER PATH

At every kilometer
every year
browbeaten old informers stand[1]
lining the land
pointing children the way
with reinforced concrete hand.

---

[1] May the reader indulge me for tinkering with Prévert's "*front borné*" in his punning allusion to the kilometer markers—"*bornes*"—familiar along the French highway landscape.

LE GRAND HOMME

Chez un tailleur de pierre
où je l'ai rencontré
il faisait prendre ses mesures
pour la postérité.

THE GREAT MAN

I once saw his eminence
in a stonecutter's shop where he
came to have his measurements
taken for posterity.

LA CÈNE

Ils sont à table
Ils ne mangent pas
Ils ne sont pas dans leur assiette
Et leur assiette se tient toute droite
Verticalement derrière leur tête.

THE LAST SUPPER

They're seated at table
They're not eating
They're not in their accustomed con*dish*on[1]
And their dishes stand upright behind their heads
In vertical position.

---

[1] Etymologically, *"être dans son assiette"* (to be in fine fettle) has little to do with the noun for "dish," but Prévert plays on the two for a little irreligious and artistic banter.

LES BELLES FAMILLES

Louis I
Louis II
Louis III
Louis IV
Louis V
Louis VI
Louis VII
Louis VIII
Louis IX
Louis X (dit le Hutin)
Louis XI
Louis XII
Louis XIII
Louis XIV
Louis XV
Louis XVI
Louis XVIII
et plus personne plus rien...
Qu'est-ce que c'est que ces gens-là
qui ne sont pas foutus
de compter jusqu'à vingt?

FINE FAMILIES

Louis I
Louis II
Louis III
Louis IV
Louis V
Louis VI
Louis VII
Louis VIII
Louis IX
Louis X (called The Quarrelsome)
Louis XI
Louis XII
Louis XIII
Louis XIV
Louis XV
Louis XVI
Louis XVIII
Louis a-plenty
but no more none but these…
What do you make of families
that can't even count to a frigging twenty?

L'ÉCOLE DES BEAUX-ARTS

Dans une boîte de paille tressée
Le père choisit une petite boule de papier
Et il la jette
Dans la cuvette
Devant ses enfants intrigués
Surgit alors
Multicolore
La grande fleur japonaise
Le nénuphar instantané
Et les enfants se taisent
Émerveillés
Jamais plus tard dans leur souvenir
Cette fleur ne pourra se faner
Cette fleur subite
Faite pour eux
A la minute
Devant eux.

THE SCHOOL OF FINE ARTS

Out of a box of braided straw
The father takes a paper ball
And lets it fall
Before each youngster's gaping jaw
And wide-eyed stare into the bowl
Then lo! that water lily Japanese
Quick as you please
Opens into an instant whole
Of many a hue and shade
The children gazed in silent awe
Nevermore will that flower fade
That blossom made
Sudden-wise
That flower grown
For them alone
Before their eyes.

QUARTIER LIBRE

J'ai mis mon képi dans la cage
et je suis sorti avec l'oiseau sur la tête
Alors
on ne salue plus
a demandé le commandant
Non
on ne salue plus
a répondu l'oiseau
Ah bon
excusez-moi je croyais qu'on saluait
a dit le commandant
Vous êtes tout excusé tout le monde peut se tromper
a dit l'oiseau.

TIME OFF

I put my soldier hat in the cage
and I went outdoors with the bird on my head
So
we don't salute anymore
asked the major
No
we don't salute anymore
answered the bird
Oh
excuse me I thought we still saluted
said the major
You're excused anyone can make a mistake
said the bird.

IMMENSE ET ROUGE

Immense et rouge
Au-dessus du grand Palais
Le soleil d'hiver apparaît
Et disparaît
Comme lui mon cœur va disparaître
Et tout mon sang va s'en aller
S'en aller à ta recherche
Mon amour
Ma beauté
Et te trouver
Là où tu es.

IMMENSE AND RED

Immense and red
Above the Grand Palais
The winter sun appears
And disappears
Like him my heart will disappear
And all my blood will be going off
Off to look for you
My love
My beauty
And to find you too
Wherever you are.

CHANSON

Quel jour sommes-nous
Nous sommes tous les jours
Mon amie
Nous sommes toute la vie
Mon amour
Nous nous aimons et nous vivons
Nous vivons et nous nous aimons
Et nous ne savons pas ce que c'est que la vie
Et nous ne savons pas ce que c'est que le jour
Et nous ne savons pas ce que c'est que l'amour.

SONG

What day are we
We're every day
My friend
We're all of life
My love
We love each other and we're living
We're living and we love each other
And we don't know what life's about
And we don't know what day's about
And we don't know what love's about.

COMPOSITION FRANÇAISE

Tout jeune Napoléon était très maigre
et officier d'artillerie
plus tard il devint empereur
alors il prit du ventre et beaucoup de pays
et le jour où il mourut il avait encore
du ventre
mais il était devenu plus petit.

FRENCH COMPOSITION

As a young man Napoleon was very skinny
and an artillery officer
later on he became emperor
then he got a big belly and lots of countries
and the day he died he still had
a big belly
but he had grown much smaller.

L'ÉCLIPSE

Louis XIV qu'on appelait aussi le Roi Soleil
était souvent assis sur une chaise percée
vers la fin de son règne
une nuit où il faisait très sombre
le Roi Soleil se leva de son lit
alla s'asseoir sur sa chaise
et disparut.

THE ECLIPSE

Louis XIV called the Sun King as well
would often sit on a chair-turned-loo
toward the end of his reign
one night when it was especially dark
the Sun King arose and got out of bed
went over and sat on his armchair-commode
and sank out of sight.[1]

---

[1] I tinker with the original slightly to preserve the sun image—arising and setting—in my translation.

CHEZ LA FLEURISTE

Un homme entre chez une fleuriste
et choisit des fleurs
la fleuriste enveloppe les fleurs
l'homme met la main à sa poche
pour chercher l'argent
l'argent pour payer les fleurs
mais il met en même temps
subitement
la main sur son cœur
et il tombe

En même temps qu'il tombe
l'argent roule à terre
et puis les fleurs tombent
en même temps que l'homme
en même temps que l'argent
et la fleuriste reste là
avec l'argent qui roule
avec les fleurs qui s'abîment
avec l'homme qui meurt
évidemment tout cela est très triste
et il faut qu'elle fasse quelque chose
la fleuriste
mais elle ne sait pas comment s'y prendre
elle ne sait pas
par quel bout commencer

Il y a tant de choses à faire
avec cet homme qui meurt
ces fleurs qui s'abîment

AT THE FLOWER SHOP

A man goes into a flower shop
and picks out some flowers
the florist lady wraps up the flowers
the man puts his hand in his pocket
to get the money
the money to pay for the flowers
but at the same time
all of a sudden
he puts his hand on his heart
and falls over

At the same time as he falls
the money rolls on the ground
and the flowers fall
at the same time as the man
at the same time as the money
and the florist lady stands there
with the money rolling around
with the flowers going bad
with the man lying dying
now obviously all that is very sad
and the florist lady
really has to do something
but she doesn't know just how to go about it
she doesn't know
just where to turn first

There's so much to take care of
so many things to do
what with that man who's dying
those flowers going bad

et cet argent
cet argent qui roule
qui n'arrête pas de rouler.

and that money
that money on the ground
that keeps rolling rolling around.

L'ÉPOPÉE

Le tombereau de l'empereur passe interminablement
Un invalide le conduit qui marche sur une main
Une main gantée de blanc
De l'autre main il tient la bride
Il a perdu ses deux jambes dans l'histoire
Il y a de cela très longtemps
Et elles se promènent là-bas
Dans l'histoire
Chacune de son côté
Et quand elles se rencontrent
Elles se donnent des coups de pied
À la guerre comme à la guerre
Qu'est-ce que vous voulez.

THE EPIC

The emperor's cart toddles by endlessly
A cripple leads it crawling on one hand
A hand gloved white
With the other hand he holds the rein
He lost both legs historically
A long time ago
And they've been carrying on
Historically
Loping along each separately
And when they meet as meet they might
They stop and kick each other too
But war is war and all is fair
So what can you do.

DIMANCHE

Entre les rangées d'arbres de l'avenue des Gobelins
Une statue de marbre me conduit par la main
Aujourd'hui c'est dimanche les cinémas sont pleins
Les oiseaux dans les branches regardent les humains
Et la statue m'embrasse mais personne ne nous voit
Sauf un enfant aveugle qui nous montre du doigt.

SUNDAY

On Avenue des Gobelins between the trees
A marble statue takes me by the hand and she's
Leading me down the avenue along and through it
Birds on the boughs ogle the human she-and-he's
It's Sunday cinemas are full of attendees
The statue kisses me but no one sees her do it
Save a blind child who points and calls attention to it.

LE JARDIN

Des milliers et des milliers d'années
Ne sauraient suffire
Pour dire
La petite seconde d'éternité
Où tu m'as embrassé
Où je t'ai embrassée
Un matin dans la lumière de l'hiver
Au Parc Montsouris à Paris
À Paris
Sur la terre
La terre qui est un astre.

THE GARDEN

Thousands and thousands of years would be
Too few to tell
Sufficiently
The little second of eternity
When you kissed me
When I kissed you
When we embraced each other too[1]
One morning in the winter light
In Paris in Parc Montsouris
Paris
A place on earth
On earth
That star in space.

---

[1] I add a line not in the original, but one occasioned by the two meanings of the French *"embrasser,"* a verb that has no single English equivalent.

L'AUTOMNE

Un cheval s'écroule au milieu d'une allée
Les feuilles tombent sur lui
Notre amour frissonne
Et le soleil aussi.

AUTUMN

A horse collapses midway down a lane
Leaves fall on him as leaves will do
Our love shudders and shakes
The sun does too.

PARIS AT NIGHT

Trois allumettes une à une allumées dans la nuit
La première pour voir ton visage tout entier
La seconde pour voir tes yeux
La dernière pour voir ta bouche
Et l'obscurité tout entière pour me rappeler tout cela
En te serrant dans mes bras.

"PARIS AT NIGHT"

Three matches one by one lit in the night
The first to see your face complete
The second one to see your eyes
The last to see your lips
And then
Darkness complete to let me think of them again
As my arms hold you hug you tight.

LE DISCOURS SUR LA PAIX

Vers la fin d'un discours extrêmement important
le grand homme d'état trébuchant
sur une belle phrase creuse
tombe dedans
et désemparé la bouche grande ouverte
haletant
montre les dents
et la carie dentaire de ses pacifiques raisonnements
met à vif le nerf de la guerre
la délicate question d'argent.

THE SPEECH ON PEACE

Reaching the end of a speech monumental
the statesman of great stature stumbling
over a fine but hollow phrase
tumbles down in it
and mumbles breathless
showing his teeth mouth open wide
next minute
the carie dental
that flaws his pro-peace argument lays bare inside
the painful nerve the "nerve of war"
(alias "money")[1] a matter to be wrangled for
in manner gentle.

---

[1] It seemed necessary to indicate (even if only tucked into a parenthesis) the common French definition of money as *"le nerf de la guerre"* (the nerve of war).

LE CONTRÔLEUR

Allons allons
Pressons
Allons allons
Voyons pressons
Il y a trop de voyageurs
Trop de voyageurs
Pressons pressons
Il y en a qui font la queue
Il y en a partout
Beaucoup
Le long du débarcadère
Ou bien dans les couloirs du ventre de leur mère
Allons allons pressons
Pressons sur la gâchette
Il faut bien que tout le monde vive
Alors tuez-vous un peu
Allons allons
Voyons
Soyons sérieux
Laissez la place
Vous savez bien que vous ne pouvez pas rester là
Trop longtemps
Il faut qu'il y en ait pour tout le monde
Un petit tour on vous l'a dit
Un petit tour du monde
Un petit tour dans le monde
Un petit tour et on s'en va
Allons allons
Pressons pressons
Soyez polis
Ne poussez pas.

THE TICKET-TAKER

Let's go let's go
Come on move along
Move move
Let's go
Come on push a little
Too many people who want to get on
Too many too many
They're standing in line
They're everywhere
They're crowding the platform waiting to take the ride
Or inside lining the walls of their mothers' womb
It's full no room
Let's go move along
Push push
A little push a little pull
Everyone needs a turn to live
Let's pull the trigger come on let her give
Kill yourselves a little
Let's go let's go
Come on let's be fair
Make room for the others
You know you just can't keep standing there
Too long much too long
There's got to be some for everyone
It's not too long is it
Just a little visit
Just a little world tour
Just a little turn round then it's over and done
Let's go let's go
Come on move along
Be polite
No pushing.

LE TEMPS PERDU

Devant la porte de l'usine
le travailleur soudain s'arrête
le beau temps l'a tiré par la veste
et comme il se retourne
et regarde le soleil
tout rouge tout rond
souriant dans son ciel de plomb
il cligne de l'œil
familièrement
Dis donc camarade Soleil
tu ne trouves pas
que c'est plutôt con
de donner une journée pareille
à un patron?

WASTED WEATHER[1]

The worker at the factory gate
stopped short as suddenly
the lovely day tugged at his coat
and as he turned his head and cast an eye
up at the sun
so round so red
and smiling in his leaden sky
he faced him gave a little wink
familiarly
So what's the story old pal Sun
don't you think
it's an asshole trick—a total loss—
to waste a day nice as this one
on a frigging boss?

---

[1] Though one will recall, even without a nod to Proust, that *"le temps perdu"* is a cliché for lost (or wasted) time, Prévert is clearly playing on the other—meteorological—meaning of the noun.

PROMENADE DE PICASSO

Sur une assiette bien ronde en porcelaine réelle
une pomme pose
Face à face avec elle
un peintre de la réalité
essaie vainement de peindre
la pomme telle qu'elle est
mais
elle ne se laisse pas faire
la pomme
elle a son mot à dire
et plusieurs tours dans son sac de pomme
la pomme
et la voilà qui tourne
dans son assiette réelle
sournoisement sur elle-même
doucement sans bouger
et comme un duc de Guise qui se déguise en bec de gaz
parce qu'on veut malgré lui lui tirer le portrait
la pomme se déguise en beau fruit déguisé
et c'est alors
que le peintre de la réalité
commence à réaliser
que toutes les apparences de la pomme sont contre lui
et
comme le malheureux indigent

PICASSO OUT STROLLING

On a very round genuine real-life porcelain plate
an apple strikes a pose
Across from her standing nose to nose
a real-life painter
struggles vainly to paint
the apple just as she is
but
she wants no part of that art of his
the apple does
she's got a lot to say in the matter
and she's got plenty of tricks packed up in her apple-sack
the apple does
and now she starts turning
ever so slightly slyly
on her real-life plate
and like a royal pretender who pretends to be
a lamppost imposter like a duc de Guise—no portraits please—
the apple pretends she's a beautiful fruit[1]
a just-pretend candy-apple
and that's when the real-life painter
begins to realize
that the apple's sham poses are doing him in
and
like the poor homeless wretch

---

[1] Many published versions of this poem replace "fruit" here with *"bruit"* (noise), but the (il)logic of the metaphor escapes me, and I doubt that it was what Prévert had in mind.

comme le pauvre nécessiteux qui se trouve soudain à la merci
de n'importe quelle association bienfaisante et charitable et
redoutable de bienfaisance de charité et de redoutabilité
le malheureux peintre de la réalité
se trouve soudain alors être la triste proie
d'une innombrable foule d'associations d'idées
Et la pomme en tournant évoque le pommier
le Paradis terrestre et Ève et puis Adam
l'arrosoir l'espalier Parmentier l'escalier
le Canada les Hespérides la Normandie la Reinette et l'Api
le serpent du jeu de Paume le serment du Jus de Pomme
et le péché originel
et les origines de l'art
et la Suisse avec Guillaume Tell
et même Isaac Newton
plusieurs fois primé à l'Exposition de la Gravitation Universelle
et le peintre étourdi perd de vue son modèle
et s'endort
C'est alors que Picasso
qui passait par là comme il passe partout
chaque jour comme chez lui
voit la pomme et l'assiette et le peintre endormi
Quelle idée de peindre une pomme

like the penniless bum thrown all at once on the mercy of some
    philanthropic and charitable and awe-inspiring philanthropy's
    and charity's and
awe-inspiration's organizations
the poor real-life painter of reality
becomes an unhappy victim suddenly
consumed in a flood of ideas unabating free-associating
And the apple turning turns to an apple tree[2]
apples apples all kinds in a row apples of myth and of history
apples of all places apples of all times
apple-expressions and apple-rhymes
and almost-rhymes apple chapel Whitechapel and *a cappella*
Sainte Chapelle Saint Jacques de Compostèle or Compostela
and applejack and apple pies the apples of his eyes and Eve in
    Earthly Paradise
then Adam too and Eve's and Adam's apple apples and loaves
    apple groves and fishes
and the Salmon on the Mount and Original Sin and art's origin
and mankind's fall and Parmentier and his potatoes—*pommes
    frites,* after all—
and William Tell and the whole Swiss nation
and Isaac Newton and the prizes he won at the Exposition of
    Universal Gravitation
and the painter struck dumb forgets all about his model
and falls asleep
Just then Picasso
comes strolling by as he strolls by everywhere
making himself quite at home every day free as you please
sees the apple and the plate and he sees the painter sleeping
Ah so
says Picasso
what a curious idea to paint an apple how very un-apeeling

dit Picasso
et Picasso mange la pomme
et la pomme lui dit Merci
et Picasso casse l'assiette
et s'en va en souriant
et le peintre arraché à ses songes
comme une dent
se retrouve tout seul devant sa toile inachevée
avec au beau milieu de sa vaisselle brisée
les terrifiants pépins de la réalité.

and Picasso eats the apple
and the apple tells him Thanks
and Picasso breaks the plate
and walks off with a smile
and the painter yanked out of his dreams
like a tooth
finds himself by his still life still unfinished as can be
alone in the midst of his smashed crockery
and the terrifying seeds of reality

---

[2] A certain amount of re-handling and re-positioning—translator's license?—has been called for to preserve the core of the many apple allusions: lexical, religious, and political. The puns in the original on the duc de Guise, for example, might refer to Jean d'Orléans, the Orleanist claimant to the throne under the name Jean III. But since he died in 1940, he was not exactly an everyday name when this poem was first published in 1944. So perhaps it is a historical reference to the ducal victim of a famous assassination in 1588. (An 1835 painting of the event in the chateau of Blois might explain the "portrait" allusion, abstruse at best.) As for Prévert's egregious pun pitting the famous *"Serment* (serpent) *du Jeu de Paume"*—the June 20, 1789 "Tennis Court Oath" of the Revolution—against the almost homophonic but virtually meaningless *"Serment du Jus de Pomme"* (Apple Juice Oath), my deformed wordplay on "apple groves / loaves and fishes" admittedly pales in comparison, despite its possibly Prévert-worthy "Salmon on the Mount"…

HISTOIRES

(1946)

CHANSON DU MOIS DE MAI

L'âne le roi et moi
Nous serons morts demain
L'âne de faim
Le roi d'ennui
Et moi d'amour

Un doigt de craie
Sur l'ardoise des jours
Trace nos noms
Et le vent dans les peupliers
Nous nomme
Ane Roi Homme

Soleil de Chiffon noir
Déjà nos noms sont effacés
Eau fraîche des Herbages
Sable des Sabliers
Rose du Rosier rouge
Chemin des Écoliers

L'âne le roi et moi
Nous serons morts demain
L'âne de faim
Le roi d'ennui
Et moi d'amour
Au mois de mai

La vie est une cerise
La mort est un noyau
L'amour un cerisier.

SONG OF THE MONTH OF MAY

The ass the king and me
Tomorrow we'll be dead
Ass from hunger
King from ennui
And me from love

A finger of chalk
On the slate of days
Traces our names
And the wind in the poplar trees
Calls us these
Ass King Man

Black rag-Sun erasing
Our names wiped clean effaced
Cool-watered Shrubberies
Sand through Hourglasses passing
Rose on the Rosebush red
And Schoolboys' dawdling pace

The ass the king and me
Tomorrow we'll be dead
Ass from hunger
King from ennui
And me from love
In the month of May

Life is a cherry
Death is a stone
And love a cherry tree

LE RUISSEAU

Beaucoup d'eau a passé sous les ponts
et puis aussi énormément de sang
Mais aux pieds de l'amour
coule un grand ruisseau blanc
Et dans les jardins de la lune
où tous les jours c'est ta fête
ce ruisseau chante en dormant
Et cette lune c'est ma tête
où tourne un grand soleil bleu
Et ce soleil c'est tes yeux.

THE STREAM[1]

The bridges arched above as water rushed
and gushing torrents flowed with blood
But at the feet of love
there streams a great white flood
And in the gardens of the moon
where each day is your special one
sleeping that stream warbles a tune
And in that moon—my head—a sun
a great blue sun rolls round the skies
The sun that is your very eyes.

---

[1] I leave it to the reader to extract a specific meaning from this lyric, typical of Prévert's surrealist inspiration.

LE LUNCH

Le maître d'hôtel noir
est pendu après la suspension
Il a osé jeté un regard
dans le décolleté
de la maîtresse de maison.

A LUNCHING[1]

The black maitre-d'
is hanging near the chandelier
He dared to sneak a little peek
down into the blouse
of the lady of the house.

---

[1] In French the word *"lunch"* is generally homonymous with *"lynch,"* as in the naturalized noun *"le lynchage"* (lynching), hence my title.

MA PETITE LIONNE

Ma petite lionne
je n'aimais pas que tu me griffes
et je t'ai livrée aux chrétiens
Pourtant je t'aimais bien
Je voudrais que tu me pardonnes
ma petite lionne.

MY LITTLE LIONESS

My little lioness
I didn't like your clawing me
so tossed you to the Christians then
Yet I still liked you nonetheless
and wish we could be friends again
my little lioness.

AU PAVILLON DE LA BOUCHERIE

Durement
coquettement piquée
dans la viande tendre de l'étal
une rose rouge de papier
hurle à la mort
en robe de bal
Un carnivore en tenue de soirée
passe devant la fleur sans la voir
ni l'entendre
Et dans le ruisseau
du sang
sur l'eau d'abord s'étale
et puis s'écoule calmement
dans la douce chaleur de la nuit
tenant un instant compagnie
au passant.

AT THE BUTCHER SHOP'S DISPLAY

Roughly
stuck in coquettish pose
into the tender flesh of the stall
a red paper rose
dressed for the ball
stands howling and baying
A carnivore in evening clothes
goes by straying near her
doesn't see her doesn't hear her
And in the gutter
blood
trickles to join the water at first
then flows with utter
calm in night's gentle heat as it
gives the passerby its company
for just a bit.

LE MÉTÉORE

Entre les barreaux des locaux disciplinaires
une orange
passe comme un éclair
et tombe dans la tinette
comme une pierre
Et le prisonnier
tout éclaboussé de merde
resplendit
tout illuminé de joie
Elle ne m'a pas oublié
Elle pense toujours à moi.

THE METEOR

Between the bars of a reformatory cell
an orange
came flying in a flash and fell
plop like a stone
into the john
And gazing at it
the prisoner shone[1]
all splattered with shit
in a blaze of ecstasy
She hasn't forgotten
She still thinks of me.

---

[1] "Shone" can be read to rhyme either with "john" or "stone," depending which of its acceptable pronunciations one prefers. Both would fit nicely.

LE TENDRE ET DANGEREUX
VISAGE DE L'AMOUR

Le tendre et dangereux
visage de l'amour
m'est apparu un soir
après un trop long jour
C'était peut-être un archer
avec son arc
ou bien un musicien
avec sa harpe
Je ne sais plus
Je ne sais rien
Tout ce que je sais
c'est qu'il m'a blessée
peut-être avec une flèche
peut-être avec une chanson
Tout ce que je sais
c'est qu'il m'a blessée
blessée au cœur
et pour toujours
Brûlante trop brûlante
blessure de l'amour.

LOVE'S DANGEROUS
AND TENDER FACE

Love's dangerous
and tender face
one evening came to me
after too long a day
Or could it be
a bowman with his bow
a singer with his harp
I don't know anymore
I don't know anything
I only know
that he wounded me
perhaps with an arrow
perhaps with a song
I only know
that he wounded me
laid low my woman's heart
eternally
Burning so burning
love's wound
love's smart.

LE BAPTÊME DE L'AIR

Cette rue
autrefois on l'appelait la rue du Luxembourg
à cause du jardin
Aujourd'hui on l'appelle la rue Guynemer
à cause d'un aviateur mort à la guerre
Pourtant
cette rue
c'est toujours la même rue
c'est toujours le même jardin
c'est toujours le Luxembourg
Avec les terrasses… les statues… les bassins
Avec les arbres
les arbres vivants
Avec les oiseaux
les oiseaux vivants
Avec les enfants
tous les enfants vivants
Alors on se demande
on se demande vraiment
ce qu'un aviateur mort vient foutre là-dedans.

THE BAPTISM OF FLIGHT

This street
its name was once Rue du Luxembourg
after the garden
Today its name is Rue Guynemer
after a pilot shot down—*c'est la guerre*—
And yet
this street
it's still the same street
it's still the same garden
it's still the Luxembourg
With the terraces... and the statues... and the pools
With the trees
trees living pat
With the birds
birds living pat
With the kids
kids all living pat
And we wonder... Ah but
we really have to wonder what
the fuck a dead pilot has to do with all that.

FIESTA

Et les verres étaient vides
et la bouteille brisée
Et le lit était grand ouvert
et la porte fermée
Et toutes les étoiles de verre
du bonheur et de la beauté
resplendissaient dans la poussière
de la chambre mal balayée
Et j'étais ivre mort
et j'étais feu de joie
et toi ivre vivante
toute nue dans mes bras.

FIESTA

And the glasses were empty
and the bottle was smashed
And the bed was wide open
and the door was shut tight
And all the stars of shattered glass
of happiness and beauty kept
twinkling with their resplendent light
over the dust of the room unswept
I was dead drunk
a bonfire flashing in the air
and you were living drunk
in my arms lying bare.

LA SAGESSE DES NATIONS

Minerve pleure
sa dent de sagesse pousse
et la guerre recommence sans cesse.

THE WISDOM OF THE NATIONS

Minerva weeps
her wisdom tooth grows
and war breaks out again and again.

LES OMBRES

Tu es là
en face de moi
dans la lumière de l'amour
Et moi
je suis là
en face de toi
avec la musique du bonheur
Mais ton ombre
sur le mur
guette tous les instants
de mes jours
et mon ombre à moi
fait de même
épiant ta liberté
Et pourtant je t'aime
et tu m'aimes
comme on aime le jour et la vie ou l'été
Mais comme les heures qui se suivent
et ne sonnent jamais ensemble
nos deux ombres se poursuivent
comme deux chiens de la même portée
détachés de la même chaîne
mais hostiles tous deux à l'amour
uniquement fidèles à leur maître
à leur maîtresse
et qui attendent patiemment
mais tremblants de détresse
la séparation des amants
qui attendent
que notre vie s'achève
et notre amour

THE SHADOWS

You're here
across from me
in the shining light of love
And me
I'm here
across from you
with happiness's music playing
But on the wall
your shadow
is spying on all
the moments of my life
and my shadow too
does quite the same
eyeing your liberty
And yet I love you
and you love me
the way one loves the daylight and life or summer
But like hours that follow each other one by one
and never sound together
our two shadows chase each other
like a brace of hounds
loosed from a single chain
but each ill-disposed to loving
faithful to none but their master
their mistress too
and who
patiently wait
but trembling with chagrin
for the lovers to draw apart
and who wait
for our lives and our love

et que nos os leur soient jetés
pour s'en saisir
et les cacher et les enfouir
et s'enfouir en même temps
sous les cendres du désir
dans les débris du temps.

to be done in
and our bones
to be flung down
to seize them and keep
them hidden to bury them deep
and bury themselves as well
beneath the ashes of desire
in time's same rubbish heap.

LE BONHEUR DES UNS

Poissons amis aimés
Amants de ceux qui furent pêchés en si grande quantité
Vous avez assisté à cette calamité
À cette chose horrible
À cette chose affreuse
À ce tremblement de terre
La pêche miraculeuse
Poissons amis aimés
Amants de ceux qui furent pêchés en si grande quantité
De ceux qui furent pêchés ébouillantés mangés
Poissons... poissons... poissons...
Comme vous avez dû rire
Le jour de la crucifixion.

ONE MAN'S BLESSING

Friend fish beloved fish
Lovers of those who got themselves fished up in droves
(Along with those loaves)[1]
You were there for that horror
That adventure devilish
That event calamitous
That shook the very earth
The catch miraculous
Friend fish beloved fish
Lovers of those who got themselves fished up in droves
And who were caught and poached and served up
So that the multitude might sup
In their affliction
Fish… fish… fish… fish…
You must have laughed to get your wish
The day of the crucifixion.

---

[1] I take the liberty of adding a line here for readers whom the religious allusion might escape.

RÊVERIE

Pauvre joueur de bilboquet[1]
A quoi penses-tu
Je pense aux filles aux mille bouquets
Je pense aux filles aux mille beaux culs.

REVERIE

Poor peg-ball player—up, down, out—
What do you think about
I think of a thousand flowering lasses
I think of a thousand lovely fair asses.

---

[1] The traditional French *"bilboquet"* consists of a stringed ball with a drilled hole, thrown out in an arc and (hopefully) caught on a peg. Originally I had made a cultural change to the yo-yo, no less French but more common to anglophone readers. During a discussion following a reading of mine, however, an anonymous young lady (whom I would acknowledge if I could) pointed out the Freudian implications of both the game and this quatrain, and I have restored the phallic *"bilboquet"* to its rightful place in Prévert's inspiration.

LE CHAT ET L'OISEAU

Un village écoute désolé
Le chant d'un oiseau blessé
C'est le seul oiseau du village
Et c'est le seul chat du village
Qui l'a à moitié dévoré
Et l'oiseau cesse de chanter
Le chat cesse de ronronner
Et de se lécher le museau
Et le village fait à l'oiseau
De merveilleuses funérailles
Et le chat qui est invité
Marche derrière le petit cercueil de paille
Où l'oiseau mort est allongé
Porté par une petite fille
Qui n'arrête pas de pleurer
Si j'avais su que cela te fasse tant de peine
Lui dit le chat
Je l'aurais mangé tout entier
Et puis je t'aurais raconté
Que je l'avais vu s'envoler
S'envoler jusqu'au bout du monde
Là-bas où c'est tellement loin
Que jamais on n'en revient
Tu aurais eu moins de chagrin
Simplement de la tristesse et des regrets

Il ne faut jamais faire les choses à moitié.

THE CAT AND THE BIRD

A village sadly listened and heard
The singing of a wounded bird
The one and only bird in town
And it's the only cat in town
That half-devoured him down at that
But all at once bird's singing stops
And cat stops purring and licking his chops
And the town makes a funeral second to none
As for the cat
Invited along with everyone
He follows behind the little straw coffin
They're carrying the bird's corpse off in
Held in the hands of a little miss
Weeping her eyes out sobbing crying
Well now what's this
The cat surprised queries the tot
If I had known you would be so chagrined
I would have eaten him on the spot
And told you I'd seen him flying
Flying aloft on the wind
Off to some land so far that never
Will he return but stay forever
You'd miss him for a while I guess
But it could well have spared you much distress

We ought not ever leave what we've begun
Half done.

RIEN À CRAINDRE

Ne craignez rien
Gens honnêtes et exemplaires
Il n'y a pas de danger
Vos morts sont bien morts
Vos morts sont bien gardés
Il n'y a rien à craindre
On ne peut vous les prendre
Ils ne peuvent se sauver
Il y a des gardiens dans les cimetières
Et puis.
Tout autour des tombes
Il y a un entourage de fer
Comme autour des lits-cages
Où dorment les enfants en bas âge
Et c'est une précaution sage
Dans son dernier sommeil
Sait-on jamais
Le mort pourrait rêver encore
Rêver qu'il est vivant
Rêver qu'il n'est plus mort
Et secouant ses draps de pierre
Se dégager
Et se pencher
Et tomber de la tombe
Comme un enfant du lit
Horreur et catacombes
Retomber dans la vie
Vous voyez cela d'ici
Tout serait remis en question

NOTHING TO FEAR

Don't be afraid
You honest souls you luminaries
There is no danger here
Your dead are very dead
Your dead are guarded well
There isn't anything to fear
They can't be snatched from you
They can't go running off
Watchmen guard the cemeteries
And round the tombs
Are grills like cribs in babies' rooms
The kind with railings you can raise to keep
Them in then lower so that they can creep
And crawl
A wise precaution all in all
Who knows if in man's final sleep
He might not dream that death is but
A dream and that
His life is what
He's living yet
Who like a tot waking in bed
Might shake free from his sheets of stone
Rise up
Lean out
Fall from the tomb gravely undead
O catacombs horror unknown
To plunge into this life once more
Everything as it was before
Everything upside down for everyone
Can't you just see it
The dead reborn

L'affection et la desolation
Et la succession
Rassurez-vous braves gens
Honnêtes et exemplaires
Vos morts ne reviendront pas
S'amuser sur la terre
Les larmes ont été versées une fois pour toutes
Et il n'y aura pas
Il n'y aura jamais plus à revenir là-dessus
Et rien dans le cimetière
Ne sera saccagé
Les pots de chrysanthèmes resteront à leur place
Et vous pourrez vaquer en toute tranquillité
L'arrosoir à la main devant le mausolée
Aux doux labeurs champêtres des éternels regrets.

Love and despair
And everywhere
Wills come undone unwrit unsworn...
Nothing to fear good folk and true
I guarantee it
You honest souls you luminaries
Your dead will not come back to you
To play life's game once tears are shed
They'll never be unshed so be it
Everything in the cemeteries
Will stay the same the dead are dead
Nothing will be wrenched out of place
The flower-pot chrysanthemums still grace
The mausoleum doors
And watering-can in hand you can feel free
To carry out with unalloyed relief
The rustic chores of your eternal grief.

ACCALMIE

Le vent
Debout
S'assoit
Sur les tuiles du toit.

LULL

Standing
The wind
Sits a while
On the rooftop tile.

LE GRAND HOMME
ET L'ANGE GARDIEN

Vous resterez là
Sentinelle
À la porte du bordel
Et vous garderez
Mon Sérieux
Moi je monte avec ces dames
Il faut bien rigoler un peu!

THE GREAT MAN
AND THE GUARDIAN ANGEL

You'll stand on guard before
The whorehouse door
And it'll
Be your job to keep safe for me
My Propriety
I'm going to go upstairs with these ladies
Everyone needs to play around a little!

MEA CULPA

C'est ma faute
C'est ma faute
C'est ma très grande faute d'orthographe
Voilà comment j'écris
Giraffe.

MEA CULPA

The fault is mine
The fault is mine
Mine is the frightful spelling gaffe
This is the way I write
Giraffe.[1]

---

[1] "Giraffe" is as commonly misspelled in English as is *"girafe"* in French. For the poet's subsequent "codicil" to this poem, see p. 395.

QUELQU'UN

Un homme sort de chez lui
C'est très tôt le matin
C'est un homme qui est triste
Cela se voit à sa figure
Soudain dans une boîte à ordures
Il voit un vieux Bottin Mondain
Quand on est triste on passe le temps
Et l'homme prend le Bottin
Le secoue un peu et le feuillette machinalement
Les choses sont comme elles sont
Cet homme si triste est triste parce qu'il s'appelle Ducon
Et il feuillette
Et continue à feuilleter
Et il s'arrête
À la page des D
Et il regarde à la colonne des D-U du...
Et son regard d'homme triste devient plus gai plus clair
Personne
Vraiment personne ne porte le même nom
Je suis le seul Ducon
Dit-il entre ses dents
Et il jette le livre s'époussette les mains
Et poursuit fièrement son petit bonhomme de chemin.

A SOMEBODY

A man leaves his place
It's early in the morning
He's a sad one you can see
By the look on his face
There in a trash can suddenly
He happens to see an old telephone book
A directory
When you're sad you pass the time
By hook or crook any way you can do it
So he picks up the book and casually
Goes flipping through it
Now the sad man is sad because his name is Twot
Flipping and skipping he stops at the T's
And runs down each column for a W-O...
And the sad man's look grows brighter don't you know
In all of these
There isn't a one
None
Really no one who's got
The same name as me
I'm the only Twot
He mutters through his teeth
And he throws the book down right where he stands
Dusts off his hands
And proudly goes ambling his own sweet way.

LES PRODIGES DE LA LIBERTÉ

Entre les dents d'un piège
La patte d'un renard blanc
Et du sang sur la neige
Le sang du renard blanc
Et des traces sur la neige
Les traces du renard blanc
Qui s'enfuit sur trois pattes
Dans le soleil couchant
Avec entre les dents
Un lièvre encore vivant.

THE WONDERS OF FREEDOM

The paw of a white fox
Clutched in steel jaws laid low
And blood of the white fox
Blood on the snow
And tracks of the white fox
Tracks on the snow
Tracks of his three paws fleeing
As the sun hangs low
And there clutched in his jaws
A hare still living though.

ON FRAPPE

Qui est là
Personne
C'est simplement mon cœur qui bat
Qui bat très fort
À cause de toi
Mais dehors
La petite main de bronze sur la porte de bois
Ne bouge pas
Ne remue pas
Ne remue pas seulement le petit bout du doigt.

SOMEONE'S KNOCKING

Who's there
No one
My pounding heart is all it was
My pounding heart and nothing more
And you're the cause
But outside on the wooden door
The little bronze hand's silent grip
Stands motionless as it
Moves not a whit
Moves not
A jot
Motionless to the merest fingertip.

LE LÉZARD

Le lézard de l'amour
S'est enfui encore une fois
Et m'a laissé sa queue entre les doigts
C'est bien fait
J'avais voulu le garder pour moi.

THE LIZARD

The lizard of love
Once more has fled my company
Left his tail in my fingers hanging free
So much for that
I'd wanted to keep him just for me.

LES CHANSONS
LES PLUS COURTES...

L'oiseau qui chante dans ma tête
Et me répète que je t'aime
Et me répète que tu m'aimes
L'oiseau au fastidieux refrain
Je le tuerai demain matin.

THE SHORTEST OF SONGS...

The bird who's singing in my head
And keeps repeating that I love you
And keeps repeating that you love me
Monotonously
Bird with his ditty ever a-borning...
I'll kill him in the morning.

LA PLAGE DES SABLES BLANCS

Oubliettes des châteaux de sable
Meurtrières fenêtres de l'oubli
Tout est toujours pareil
Et cependant tout a changé
Tu étais nue dans le soleil
Tu étais nue tu te baignais
Les galets roulent avec la mer
Et toujours toujours j'entendrai
Leur doux refrain de pierres heureuses
Leur gai refrain de pierres mouillées
Déchirant refrain des vacances
Perdu dans les vagues du souvenir
Déchirants souvenirs de l'enfance
Brûlée vive par le désir
Merveilleux souvenir de l'enfance
Éblouie par le plaisir.

THE WHITE SAND BEACH

Sand castles' dismal dungeon holds
Window-slits of forgotten past
It's all the same yet everything
Has changed and nothing has held fast
You lay there naked in the sun
You bathed there naked in the sea
The flat stones still roll in the tide
And ever ever shall sing to me
Their joyous stone-refrain nor yet
Shall I forget the gay refrain
Of stones' wet frolics or vacation's pain
Lost in the waves of memory
Painful these childhood memories
A childhood burned alive in its desire
Wonder-filled childhood memories these
Childhood dazzled by pleasure's fire.

LES DERNIERS SACREMENTS

Noyé dans les grandes eaux de la misère
Qui suintent horriblement
Le long des murs de sa chambre sordide
Un mourant
Livide abandonné et condamné
Aperçoit
Dans l'ombre de la veilleuse
Promenée et bercée par le vent
Contre le mur suintant
Une lueur vivante et merveilleuse
La flamme heureuse des yeux aimés
Et il entend
Distinctement
En mourant
Dans l'éclatant silence de la chambre mortuaire
Les plus douces paroles de l'amour retrouvé
Dites par la voix même de la femme tant aimée
Et la chambre un instant s'éclaire
Comme jamais palais ne fut éclairé
Il y a le feu
Disent les voisins
Ils se précipitent
Et ne voient rien
Rien d'autre qu'un homme seul
Couché dans des draps sales
Et souriant
Malgré le vent d'hiver
Qui entre dans la chambre

THE LAST RITES

Drowning in the gushing waves of poverty
Misery oozing loathsomely[1]
Out of the walls of his squalid room
A dying man
Alone and ghastly pale with no reprieve
Perceives
In the shadow cast by his lamp
And swaying cradled by the wind
Against the sweating wall
A wonderfully life-filled light
The happy flame of eyes once dearly loved
And clearly he can hear
Lying
Dying in the bursting silence of the deathbed room
The sweetest words of a recovered love
Spoken by the beloved's very voice
And the room grows bright for a moment
Through the gloom
Brighter even than a palace full of light
It's on fire
Shout the neighbors
And they rush to have a look
But there's nothing to see
Only a man lying all alone
In grimy sheets
And smiling
Despite the winter blast
That blows into the room

Par les carreaux cassés
Cassés par la misère
Et par le temps.

Through broken-glassed panes
Broken by poverty
And weathered by time.[2]

---

[1] I don't avoid Prévert's seeming contradiction here, juxtaposing *"grandes eaux"* (torrents) with the verb *"suinter"* (to ooze), though I try to minimize it.

[2] Though *"le temps"* means both "time" and "weather," I suspect Prévert intends the former here but tip my hat to the latter in passing.

TOILE DE FOND

Assis
Près du lit défait
L'enfant du défunt
Près de feu son père
Feint de faire du feu
Et debout
Près de l'enfant fou
Sous-alimenté et décalcifié
Près de l'enfant fou et du père glacé
Un prêtre parle de l'enfer
Et l'oiseau de la maison
L'oiseau de la masure
L'oiseau de la misère
L'oiseau qui meurt de faim
Dans sa cage de fer
Siffle qu'il s'en fout
Que c'est rien la faim
Que c'est rien le feu
Que c'est rien le fer
Et que cela ne vaut pas la peine de s'en faire
De s'en faire une miette
Une miette de pain
Une miette de faim
Une miette de fer
Et puis crève à son tour
Et sifflotant et sanglotant
Éclatant de rire hurlant aboyant
L'enfant fou tourne en rond
Autour de la cage
En jouant du tambour
Et puis tourne aussi tout autour du lit

BACKDROP

Seated
Beside the unmade bed
The dead man's son
Beside his sire
Living of late but lately dead
Would fain begin
To build a fire
Feigns it begun indeed and done
Standing beside
The frigid father of the lad
Mad underfed decalcified
A priest begins to spell
The tales of hell
And the household bird unfed
Hovel bird now all but dead
Poverty bird foully bred
In iron cage opens his trap
Chirps that he doesn't give a crap
That hunger iron flame aren't worth a crumb
A crumb of hunger iron bread
A crumb of worry wearisome
Then turns and croaks falls very dead
Now sobbing
Howling
Whistling
Growling
Circling about beating a drum
The mad lad chortles round the bed
The rusting rotting cage where what
Was once his father starts to rot
Miserably

Autour du lit-cage rouillé et pourri
Où le peu qui reste du père
Mort de fatigue de faim et de misère
Se corrompt
Misérablement
Le prêtre alors ouvre la fenêtre
Miserere miserere
Et l'aurore aux doigts de fée apparaît
Et de ses doigts de fée
Délicatement
Se bouche le nez.

Dead of fatigue hunger and misery
The priest opens the window then
One miserere
One amen
And as the faerie-fingered dawn arose
With no less faerie-fingers he
Delicately
Will hold his nose.

COMME PAR MIRACLE

Comme par miracle
Des oranges aux branches d'un oranger
Comme par miracle
Un homme s'avance
Mettant comme par miracle
Un pied devant l'autre pour marcher
Comme par miracle
Une maison de pierre blanche
Derrière lui sur la terre est posée
Comme par miracle
L'homme s'arrête au pied de l'oranger
Cueille une orange l'épluche et la mange
Jette la peau au loin et crache les pépins
Apaisant comme par miracle
Sa grande soif du matin
Comme par miracle
L'homme sourit
Regardant le soleil qui se lève
Et qui luit
Comme par miracle
Et l'homme ébloui rentre chez lui
Et retrouve comme par miracle
Sa femme endormie
Émerveillé
De la voir si jeune si belle
Et comme par miracle
Nue dans le soleil
Il la regarde
Et comme par miracle elle se réveille
Et lui sourit
Comme par miracle il la caresse

QUITE MIRACULOUSLY

Quite miraculously
Oranges on the branches of an orange-tree
Quite miraculously
Along comes a man
Walking quite miraculously
Placing one foot in front of the other
Quite miraculously
A white stone house
Stands on the land behind him
Quite miraculously
The man stops under the orange-tree
Picks an orange peels it eats it
Tosses the peel away spits out the seeds
And satisfies quite miraculously
His great morning thirst
The man smiles a smile
Looks at the sun that all the while
Is rising and shining
Quite miraculously
And dazzled by its brightness he
Goes back inside and quite miraculously
Gazing in wonder
He finds sleeping there
In the sun
His woman lying bare
And seeing her so young so fair
He looks at her
And quite miraculously she wakes
And gives him a smile
Quite miraculously he gives her a caress
And quite miraculously silent acquiescer

Et comme par miracle elle se laisse caresser
Alors comme par miracle
Des oiseaux de passage passent
Qui passent comme cela
Comme par miracle
Des oiseaux de passage qui s'en vont vers la mer
Volant très haut
Au-dessus de la maison de pierre
Où l'homme et la femme
Comme par miracle
Font l'amour
Des oiseaux de passage au-dessus du jardin
Où comme par miracle l'oranger berce ses oranges
Dans le vent du matin
Jetant comme par miracle son ombre sur la route
Sur la route on un prêtre s'avance
Le nez dans son bréviaire le bréviaire dans les mains
Et le prêtre marchant sur la pelure d'orange jetée
    par l'homme au loin
Glisse et tombe
Comme un prêtre qui glisse sur une pelure d'orange
    et qui tombe sur une route
Un beau matin.

She lets him caress her
Then quite miraculously
Birds of passage fly by
Passing by just like that
Quite miraculously
Birds of passage flying on their way to the sea
Flying very high
Over the stone house high above
Where the man and his woman
Are lying making love
Birds of passage above the garden
Where quite miraculously
The orange-tree's
Branches are cradling the morning breeze
And their oranges cast quite miraculously
Their shade on the road
The road where a priest is making his way
His nose in his missal his missal in his hands
And the priest will step on the orange peel that the
    man tossed away
Will slip and fall
Quite like any priest at all who slips on an orange peel
    and falls on the road
On any fine day.

LE FUSILLÉ

Les fleurs les jardins les jets d'eau les sourires
Et la douceur de vivre
Un homme est là par terre et baigne dans son sang
Les souvenirs les fleurs les jets d'eau les jardins
Les rêves enfantins
Un homme est là par terre comme un paquet sanglant
Les fleurs les jets d'eau les jardins les souvenirs
Et la douceur de vivre
Un homme est là par terre comme un enfant dormant.

SHOT DEAD

Flowers gardens jetting streams smiles all round
And the sweetness of living
A man lies bathing in his blood there on the ground
Memories flowers gardens jetting streams
Childhood dreams
A man lies on the ground there like a bloody heap
Flowers jetting streams gardens memories found
And the sweetness of living
A man lies on the ground there like a child asleep.

LE GARDIEN DU PHARE
AIME TROP LES OISEAUX

Des oiseaux par milliers volent vers les feux
par milliers ils tombent par milliers ils se cognent
par milliers aveuglés par milliers assommés
par milliers ils meurent

Le gardien ne peut supporter des choses pareilles
les oiseaux il les aime trop
alors il dit Tant pis je m'en fous!

Et il éteint tout

Au loin un cargo fait naufrage
un cargo venant des îles
un cargo chargé d'oiseaux
des milliers d'oiseaux des îles
des milliers d'oiseaux noyés.

THE LIGHTHOUSE KEEPER
LOVES BIRDS TOO MUCH

Birds by the thousands fly toward the light
by the thousands they crash by the thousands they fall
by the thousands blinded by the thousands smashed
by the thousands they die

The lighthouse keeper can't stand for such a thing
he loves birds too much
and he says Too bad I don't give a shit!

He extinguishes it

Off in the distance a freighter goes down
a freighter from the tropics
a freighter filled with birds
thousands and thousands of birds from the tropics
thousands and thousands of birds all drown.

ADRIEN

Adrien ne fais pas la mauvaise tête!
Reviens!
Adrien ne fais pas la mauvaise tête!
Reviens!
La boule de neige
que tu m'avais jetée
à Chamonix
l'hiver dernier
je l'ai gardée
Elle est sur la cheminée
près de la couronne de mariée
de feu ma pauvre mère
qui mourut assassinée
par défunt mon père
qui mourut guillotiné
un triste matin d'hiver
ou de printemps...
J'ai eu des torts j'en conviens
je suis restée
de longues années
sans rentrer
à la maison
Mais je te l'ai toujours caché
c'est que j'étais en prison!
J'ai eu des torts j'en conviens
souvent je battais le chien
mais je t'aimais bien!...

ADRIEN

Adrien don't be so damn stand-offish!
Don't stay away!
Adrien don't be so damn stand-offish!
Don't stay away!
The snowball that you threw at me
at Chamonix
one winter day last year
I've kept above the fireplace here
one souvenir next to another
the bridal wreath of my late mother
killed by papa now dead as well—
who one sad winter morning fell
prey to the guillotine poor thing
or was it spring...
I had my faults yes I confess
Oh yes I know it seemed as though
I'd left forever
gone for years and years because
the women's jail is where I was![1]
I never let you know
why upset you
I had my faults yes I confess
I beat the dog treated him rough
but still I liked you well enough!...

Adrien ne fais pas la mauvaise tête!
Reviens!
Et Brin d'osier
ton petit fox-terrier
qui est crevé
la semaine dernière
je l'ai gardé!
Il est dans le frigidaire
et quand parfois j'ouvre la porte
pour prendre de la bière
je vois la pauvre bête morte
Ça me désespère!
Pourtant c'est moi qui l'ai fait
un soir pour passer le temps
en t'attendant...
Adrien ne fais pas la mauvaise tête!
Reviens!
De la tour Saint-Jacques
je me suis jetée
avant-hier
je me suis tuée
à cause de toi
Hier on m'a enterrée
dans un très joli cimetière
et je pensais à toi
Et ce soir je suis revenue
dans l'appartement
où tu te promenais nu
du temps que j'étais vivante
et je t'attends...

Adrien ne fais pas la mauvaise tête!
Reviens!
J'ai eu des torts j'en conviens

Adrien don't be so damn stand-offish!
Don't stay away!
And Brind'osier your terrier
who up and croaked the other day
I've kept him too for you
the more the merrier
he's in the frigidaire
And when I open up the door
to get a beer and find him there
all frozen stiff
really it breaks my heart in two
It's not as if
someone else laid him low... No I'm
the one I admit it[2]
the one who did it
to pass the time
while I waited for you...
Adrien don't be so damn stand-offish!
Don't stay away!
Day before yesterday I took a climb
up to the top of the Tour Saint-Jacques[3]
and because of you
I jumped down dead alas alack
Next day they pack me away in a very
pretty cemetery
Tonight I came back
to the apartment where
you used to go bare
when I was still living
and I wait for you there...

Adrien don't be so damn stand-offish!
Don't stay away!
I had my faults yes I confess

je suis restée de longues années
sans rentrer à la maison
Mais je te l'ai toujours caché
c'est que j'étais en prison!
J'ai eu des torts j'en conviens
souvent je battais le chien
mais je t'aimais bien!…

Adrien ne fais pas la mauvaise tête!
Reviens!

Oh yes I know it seemed as though
I'd left forever
gone for years and years because
the women's jail is where I was!
I never let you know
why upset you!
I had my faults yes I confess
I beat the dog treated him rough
but still I liked you well enough!...

Adrien don't be so damn stand-offish!
Don't stay away!

---

[1] As elsewhere, I have seen fit to add a line, discreetly I hope, to establish the speaker's gender, obvious in the French.

[2] I hope the reader will excuse the imperfect rhyme of "did it / admit it" on the grounds that a woman who kills dogs *(inter alia)* is probably not too scrupulous with her speech and would not resist the sloppy phonetic slurring of intervocalic *t* to *d*.

[3] On the corner of Rue de Rivoli and Boulevard de Sébastopol, the Tour Saint-Jacques, dating from the first decades of the 16th century, is the only part of the church of Saint-Jacques de Compostelle (also known as L'Église de la Boucherie) still standing. Its height—fifty-seven meters—made it ideal for Pascal's experiments on atmospheric pressure, as a statue of him at its base attests.

IL FAUT PASSER LE TEMPS

À Agnès Capri

On croit que c'est facile
de ne rien faire du tout
au fond c'est difficile
c'est difficile comme tout
il faut passer le temps
c'est tout un travail
il faut passer le temps
c'est un travail de titan

Ah!
du matin au soir
je ne faisais rien
rien
ah! quelle drôle de chose
du matin au soir
du soir au matin
je faisais la même chose
rien!
je ne faisais rien
j'avais les moyens
ah! quelle triste histoire
j'aurais pu tout avoir
oui
ce que j'aurais voulu
si je l'avais voulu
je l'aurais eu
mais je n'avais envie de rien
rien

YOU'VE GOT TO PASS THE TIME

for Agnès Capri[1]

You think there's nothing easier
to do than to do nothing well you
don't know how hard it is you err
there's nothing harder let me tell you
you've got to pass the time get through it
and that's a most difficult task
you've got to pass the time get through it
only a Titan's strength can do it

Ah!
dawn to dark
I used to do
nothing
ah! what odd carryings-on
dawn to dark
dark to dawn
I'd do the same thing
nothing!
not a thing
I had the means to do it
ah! what a tale of dreariness
I could have had everything
yes
everything I wanted
if I'd wanted anything
it could have been mine
but I didn't want a thing
nothing
not a thing

Un jour pourtant je vis un chien
ce chien qui me plut je l'eus
c'était un grand chien
un chien de berger
mais la pauvre bête
comme elle s'ennuyait
s'ennuyait d' son maître
un vieil Écossais
j'ai acheté son maître
j'avais les moyens
ah!
quel drôle d'écho
oh!
quel drôle d'Écossais c'était
que le berger de mon chien
toute la journée il pleurait
toute la nuit il sanglotait
ah!
c'était tout à fait insensé
l'Écossais dépérissait
il ne voulait rien entendre
il parlait même de se pendre
J'aime mieux mes moutons
chantait-il en écossais
et le chien aboyait
en l'entendant chanter
j'avais les moyens
j'achetai les moutons
je les mis dans mon salon
alors ils broutèrent mes tapis
et puis ils crevèrent d'ennui
et dans la tombe

Then one day I saw a hound
a hound that I found
quite to my liking and I kept him
a big hound because
a shepherd's hound was he
but the poor beast just pined
and pined for his master constantly
an old Scot he was
so I up and presently bought him his master
I had the means to do it
ah!
to do it! to do it![2]
oh!
my hound's odd old Scot
could not could not
but rue it rue it rue it
his sobs echoed all day
all night he wept
ah!
the old Scot kept
just wasting away
he paid no mind
to what I opined
he even said
he would hang himself dead
ah! it wasn't pretty
I'd rather be
with my sheep said he
singing a Scottish ditty
and the hound couldn't keep
from howling when he'd coo it
so presently

l'Écossais les suivit
ah!
et le chien aussi

C'est alors que je partis en croisiére

Pour-me-calmer mes-petits-nerfs.

I up and bought his sheep
I had the means to do it
and put them in my living-room
they grazed on my carpets
then croaked from ennui
and quickly found
themselves in the tomb
the Scot too soon knew it
ah!
so did the hound

And I go on a cruise in hopes that it'll

Settle my unstrung nerves a little.

---

[1] Agnès Capri was one of the various popular singers who—along with Juliette Greco, Edith Piaf, Yves Montand, et al.—popularized song-settings of a number of Prévert's poems.

[2] My rather elaborate rendition aims to suggest at least the spirit of the untranslatable wordplay presented by *echo / Écossais*.

EMBRASSE-MOI

C'était dans un quartier de la ville Lumière
Où il fait toujours noir où il n'y a jamais d'air
Et l'hiver comme l'été là c'est toujours l'hiver
Elle était dans l'escalier
Lui à côté d'elle elle à côté de lui
C'était la nuit
Ça sentait le soufre
Car on avait tué des punaises dans l'après-midi
Et elle lui disait
Ici il fait noir
Il n'y a pas d'air
L'hiver comme l'été c'est toujours l'hiver
Le soleil du bon Dieu ne brill' pas de notr' côté
Il a bien trop à faire dans les riches quartiers
Serre-moi dans tes bras
Embrasse-moi
Embrasse-moi longtemps
Embrasse-moi
Plus tard il sera trop tard
Notre vie c'est maintenant
Ici on crèv' de tout
De chaud de froid
On gèle on étouffe
On n'a pas d'air
Si tu cessais de m'embrasser
Il me semble que j' mourrais étouffée
T'as quinze ans j'ai quinze ans
À nous deux on a trente
À trente ans on n'est plus des enfants
On a bien l'âge de travailler

HUG ME KISS ME[1]

In the City of Light in a quarter where
It's always dark where there is no air
And it's winter even in summer there
It was night
And on the stair she was standing
She next to him he next to her
The smell of sulfur was all around
From the bedbugs people had killed that day
And she would say
There is no light
There is no air
It's winter even in summer here
Good God doesn't shine his sun where we're found
It has too much work I fear shining down
On the rich parts of town
So hug me kiss me
Hug me strong
Kiss me long
Later will be too late for all this
Our life is now
Here everything is death
The heat the cold
We freeze we smother
No air no breath
If you don't hug me kiss me
I know I'll choke and die
You're fifteen so am I
Each one with the other
Together we make thirty
And at thirty we're no kids
We're old enough to work

On a bien celui de s'embrasser
Plus tard il sera trop tard
Notre vie c'est maintenant
Embrasse-moi!

We're old enough to hug and kiss
Later will be too late for all this
Our life is now
So hug me kiss me!

LES BRUITS DE LA NUIT

Vous dormez sur vos deux oreilles
Comme on dit
Moi je me promène et je veille dans la nuit
Je vois des ombres j'entends des cris
Drôles de cris
Vous dormez sur vos deux oreilles
Comme on dit
C'est un chien qui hurle à la mort
C'est un chat qui miaule à l'amour
Un ivrogne perdu dans un corridor
Un fou sur son toit qui joue du tambour
J'entends aussi le rire d'une fille
Qui pour satisfaire le client
Simule la joie simule le plaisir
Et sur le lit se renverse en hurlant
Vous dormez sur vos deux oreilles
Comme on dit
Mais soudain le client prend peur
Dans la nuit il crie comme chez le dentiste
Mais c'est beaucoup plus sinistre
De dessous le lit un homme est sorti
Et tout doucement s'approche de lui
Vous dormez sur vos deux oreilles
Comme on dit
Et le client tourne de l'œil dans la nuit
Pauvre homme qu'un autre homme assomme
Pour une petite question d'argent
Pour une malheureuse petite somme
Peut-être quatre cinq ou six cents francs

NOISES IN THE NIGHT[1]

You sleep deep and you sleep tight
Like they say
Myself I'm wide awake and make my way
Through the night
I see shadows I hear cries
Strange odd cries
You sleep deep and you sleep tight
Like they say
Hound baying at some death-to-come
Cat meowing lusty lover caterwauls
Drunkard wandering round the halls
Rooftop madman pounding on a drum
And I hear a laughing whore
Howling bedded on her back
Faking pleasure more and more
To give a client what he's paying for
You sleep deep and you sleep tight
Like they say
Client suddenly takes fright
Screams one of those dentist screams
That pierce the night like pulling teeth
But fiercer and more chill it seems
A man from underneath the bed
Appears approaches stealthily
You sleep deep and you sleep tight
Like they say
In the night client kicks the bucket dead
Man pummeled by another thanks
To some absurdly piddling sum
Maybe four five six hundred francs
You sleep deep and you sleep tight

Vous dormez sur vos deux oreilles
Comme on dit
Et le client tourne de l'œil dans la nuit
Demain sa famille prendra le deuil
C'est tout cuit
Vous dormez sur vos deux oreilles
Bonne nuit.

Like they say
In the night client lies dead
Tomorrow will his family come
To mourn and that
Is where we're at
You sleep deep and you sleep tight
Good night.

_____

[1] This is one of a number of Prévert's poems set to music by Joseph Kosma. In translating it, however, I treat it strictly as a poem, with no attempt to "fit" my text to the rhythms of the song.

UN BEAU MATIN

Il n'avait peur de personne
Il n'avait peur de rien
Mais un matin un beau matin
Il croit voir quelque chose
Mais il dit Ce n'est rien
Et il avait raison
Avec sa raison sans nul doute
Ce n'était rien
Mais le matin ce même matin
Il croit entendre quelqu'un
Et il ouvrit la porte
Et il la referma en disant Personne
Et il avait raison
Avec sa raison sans nul doute
Il n'y avait personne
Mais soudain il eut peur
Et il comprit qu'il était seul
Mais qu'il n'était pas tout seul
Et c'est alors qu'il vit
Rien en personne devant lui.

ONE FINE MORNING

He was afraid of no one
He was afraid of nothing
But one morning one fine morning
He thinks he sees something
But he says It's nothing
And he was right
Right with his rightful reason quite
It was nothing
But that morning that same morning
He thinks he hears someone
And he opened the door
And he closed it saying No one
And he was right
Right with his rightful reason quite
There was no one
But suddenly he grew afraid because
He realized how alone he was
But not all alone
It was then that he saw him
And couldn't ignore him
That nothing in person standing before him.

CHANSON DU VITRIER

Comme c'est beau
ce qu'on peut voir comme ça
à travers le sable à travers le verre
à travers les carreaux
tenez regardez par exemple
comme c'est beau
ce bûcheron
là-bas au loin
qui abat un arbre
pour faire des planches
pour le menuisier
qui doit faire un grand lit
pour la petite marchande de fleurs
qui va se marier
avec l'allumeur de réverbères
qui allume tous les soirs les lumières
pour que le cordonnier puisse voir clair
en réparant les souliers du cireur
qui brosse ceux du rémouleur
qui affûte les ciseaux du coiffeur
qui coupe le ch'veu au marchand d'oiseaux
qui donne ses oiseaux à tout le monde
pour que tout le monde soit de bonne humeur.

THE GLAZIER'S SONG

How fair how grand
all the things you can see
through the window panes
made of glass made of sand
for instance take a look out there
how fair how grand
that woodsman with his axe
who hacks down a tree
to turn into boards
that the carpenter takes
and makes into a bed
for the little flower-lass
who's going to wed
the lamplighter who
lights the streetlamps each night
so the cobbler can see as best he might
to do what he has to do to repair
the shoes of the bootblack who's going to wax
and polish the ones the blade-grinder will wear
who sharpens the scissors of the coiffeur
who cuts the hair of the bird-fancier
who gives birds away to one and all free
to raise everyone's spirits and spread jollity.

CHANSON POUR LES ENFANTS L'HIVER

Dans la nuit de l'hiver
galope un grand homme blanc
galope un grand homme blanc

C'est un bonhomme de neige
avec une pipe en bois
un grand bonhomme de neige
poursuivi par le froid

Il arrive au village
il arrive au village
voyant de la lumière
le voilà rassuré

Dans une petite maison
il entre sans frapper
Dans une petite maison
il entre sans frapper
et pour se réchauffer
et pour se réchauffer
s'asseoit sur le poêle rouge
et d'un coup disparaît
ne laissant que sa pipe
au milieu d'une flaque d'eau
ne laissant que sa pipe
et puis son vieux chapeau...

CHILDREN'S WINTER SONG[1]

On a dark winter night
a white fat man went racing
a white fat man went racing

A snowman was our gent
sporting a pipe of wood
and as the cold kept chasing
he ran fast as he could

And when he reached the town
and when he reached the town
he saw a little light
and took heart at the sight

He didn't knock but went
inside the house and stood
He didn't knock but went
inside thinking he would
warm himself up thereat
warm himself up thereat
on the hot stove sat down
melted lickety-split
puddling now on the floor
our snowman is no more
only a pipe... that's that...
a pipe and his old hat...

---

[1] With no apparent music for this "song" to conform to, I give free rein to my
rather free version—perhaps both freer and more formal than Prévert's, though
without violating his spirit.

EN SORTANT DE L'ÉCOLE

En sortant de l'école
nous avons rencontré
un grand chemin de fer
qui nous a emmenés
tout autour de la terre
dans un wagon doré
Tout autour de la terre
nous avons rencontré
la mer qui se promenait
avec tous ses coquillages
ses îles parfumées
et puis ses beaux naufrages
et ses saumons fumés
Au-dessus de la mer
nous avons rencontré
la lune et les étoiles
sur un bateau à voiles
partant pour le Japon
et les trois mousquetaires des cinq doigts de la main
tournant la manivelle d'un petit sous-marin
plongeant au fond des mers
pour chercher des oursins
Revenant sur la terre
nous avons rencontré
sur la voie de chemin de fer
une maison qui fuyait
fuyait tout autour de la terre
fuyait tout autour de la mer

FRESH OUT OF SCHOOL

Fresh out of school we found
a train that presently
about the wide world round
transported us as we
rode in a coach of gold
for high adventure bound
And as the great train rolled
about the wide world round
soon we came to the sea
and found it leisurely
strolling mid shells untold
strewn roundabout and mid
its perfumed isles renowned
and the fine wrecks its waters hid
smoked salmon too (I swear)—[1]
delicacy that bid
be on our bill-of-fare
The rolling sea was crowned
by moon and stars as we
sailed on our sail-borne spree
for Japan's islands bound
Then with a fist five-fingered—sacrosanct
symbol Three Musketeers' of sorts—we cranked[2]
a little submarine
diving to hunt sea urchins deep
betwixt between
And rising back to ground
on the train's track we found
a house before us that would keep
fleeing fleeing the wide world round
fleeing fleeing about the sea

fuyait devant l'hiver
qui voulait l'attraper
Mais nous sur notre chemin de fer
on s'est mis à rouler
rouler derrière l'hiver
et on l'a écrasé
et la maison s'est arrêtée
et le printemps nous a salués
C'était lui le garde-barrière
et il nous a bien remerciés
et toutes les fleurs de toute la terre
soudain se sont mises à pousser
pousser à tort et à travers
sur la voie du chemin de fer
qui ne voulait plus avancer
de peur de les abîmer
Alors on est revenu à pied
à pied tout autour de la terre
à pied tout autour de la mer
tout autour du soleil
de la lune et des étoiles
À pied à cheval en voiture et en bateau à voiles.

fleeing from winter stubbornly
striving to catch it as it fled
But on our train we plied ahead
gave chase to winter's villainy
defied and smashed it utterly
and the house spared from death
could stop and catch its breath
Spring thanked us for our victory—
spring was the crossing-guard you see—
and suddenly the land lay spread
with flowers from the wide world round
springing sprouting over the ground
abounding lush unlimited
between the tracks beside before
behind everywhere more and more
and the train dared not move ahead
lest they be crushed and left for dead
And so we ventured homeward-bound
on foot about the wide world round
on foot about the seas' vast sprawl
about the sun the moon
the heavens starlight-strewn
By foot by horse by autocar by sail and all.

---

[1] For the reader possibly unfamiliar with the delicacy, I add a phrase to the intentional banality of Prévert's tongue-in-cheek (and rhyme-dictated?) allusion to smoked salmon.

[2] I take the liberty of capitalizing the famous characters to emphasize the idea of power and daring implied in the image of the fist.

SCENE DE LA VIE
DES ANTILOPES

En Afrique, il existe beaucoup d'antilopes; ce sont des animaux charmants et très rapides à la course.

Les habitants de l'Afrique sont les hommes noirs, mais il y a aussi des hommes blancs; ceux-ci sont de passage, ils viennent pour faire des affaires, et ils ont besoin que les Noirs les aident; mais les Noirs aiment mieux danser que construire des routes ou des chemins de fer; c'est un travail très dur pour eux et qui souvent les fait mourir.

Quand les Blancs arrivent, souvent les Noirs se sauvent, les Blancs les attrapent au lasso, et les Noirs sont obligés de faire le chemin de fer ou la route, et les Blancs les appellent des « travailleurs volontaires ».

Et ceux qu'on ne peut pas attraper parce qu'ils sont trop loin et que le lasso est trop court, ou parce qu'ils courent trop vite, on les attaque avec le fusil, et c'est pour ça que quelquefois une balle perdue dans la montagne tue une pauvre antilope endormie.

Alors, c'est la joie chez les Blancs et chez les Noirs aussi, parce que d'habitude les Noirs sont très mal nourris. Tout le monde redescend vers le village en criant:

—Nous avons tué une antilope.

Et ils en font beaucoup de musique.

Les hommes noirs tapent sur des tambours et allument de grands feux, les hommes blancs les regardent danser, le lendemain ils écrivent à leurs amis: « Il y a eu un grand tam-tam, c'était tout à fait réussi! »

En haut, dans la montagne, les parents et les camarades de l'antilope se regardent sans rien dire... Ils sentent qu'il est arrivé quelque chose...

...Le soleil se couche et chacun des animaux se demande, sans oser élever la voix pour ne pas inquiéter les autres: « Où a-t-elle pu aller, elle avait dit qu'elle serait rentrée à neuf heures... pour le dîner! »

SCENE IN THE LIFE
OF THE ANTELOPES

In Africa, there are lots of antelopes; they're delightful animals and very fleet of foot.

The inhabitants of Africa are the black men, but there are white men there also. the latter are just passing through, on business, and they need the Blacks to help them; but the Blacks would rather dance than build roads or railways; it's a very hard job for them and one that often does them in.

When the Whites show up the Blacks often go running away. The Whites lasso them, and the Blacks are obliged to build the railway or the road, and the Whites call them "volunteer workers."

And the ones that can't be caught—because they're too far off and the lasso is too short, or because they run too fast—are hunted down with rifles, and that's the reason why sometimes a stray bullet, up on the mountain, will kill a poor antelope who's lying asleep.

Then the Whites break out in joyous huzzahs, and the Blacks as well, because the Blacks are usually very ill fed. And everyone goes tramping back down to the village, shouting:

"We've killed an antelope."

And they make a lot of music.

The black men beat drums and light great fires, the white men watch them dance, and the next day they write to their friends: "There was lots of tomtom beating, and it was very nice!"

Up on the mountain, the relatives and friends of the antelope look at each other without a word... They can feel that something has happened...

Eventually the sun goes down and all of the animals ask themselves, without daring raise their voices so as not to worry the others: "Where could she have gone? She said she would be back by nine o'clock... for dinner!"[1]

Une des antilopes, immobile sur un rocher, regarde le village, très loin tout en bas, dans la vallée; c'est un tout petit village, mais il y a beaucoup de lumière et des chants et des cris… un feu de joie.

Un feu de joie chez les hommes, l'antilope a compris, elle quitte son rocher et va retrouver les autres et dit :

— Ce n'est plus la peine de l'attendre, nous pouvons dîner sans elle…

Alors toutes les autres antilopes se mettent à table, mais personne n'a faim, c'est un très triste repas.

One of the antelopes, standing motionless on a cliff, looks down at the village, far off, in the valley; it's a very small village, but there's a lot of light, and shouts, and singing... a bonfire.

Men and a bonfire... The antelope understands, gets down from the cliff and goes back to the others, saying:

"No need to wait dinner for her, we can eat without her..."

Then all the other antelopes sit down at the table, but no one is hungry, and it's a very sad meal.

---

[1] We can only guess at the sex of the antelope in question. Its grammatical gender makes it feminine. I have kept it such with a fifty percent chance of being right.

LE DROMADAIRE MÉCONTENT

Un jour, il y avait un jeune dromadaire qui n'était pas content du tout.

La veille, il avait dit à ses amis: « Demain, je sors avec mon père et ma mère, nous allons entendre une conférence, voilà comme je suis, moi! »

Et les autres avaient dit: « Oh, oh, il va entendre une conférence, c'est merveilleux », et lui n'avait pas dormi de la nuit tellement il était impatient et voilà qu'il n'était pas content parce que la conférence n'était pas du tout ce qu'il avait imaginé: il n'y avait pas de musique et il était déçu, il s'ennuyait beaucoup, il avait envie de pleurer.

Depuis une heure trois quarts un gros monsieur parlait. Devant le gros monsieur, il y avait un pot à eau et un verre à dents sans la brosse et de temps en temps, le monsieur versait de l'eau dans le verre, mais il ne se lavait jamais les dents et, visiblement irrité, il parlait d'autre chose, c'est-à-dire des dromadaires et des chameaux.

Le jeune dromadaire souffrait de la chaleur, et puis sa bosse le gênait beaucoup; elle frottait contre le dossier du fauteuil; il était très mal assis, il remuait.

Alors sa mère lui disait: « Tiens-toi tranquille, laisse parler le monsieur », et elle lui pinçait la bosse. Le jeune dromadaire avait de plus en plus envie de pleurer, de s'en aller…

Toutes les cinq minutes, le conférencier répétait: « Il ne faut surtout pas confondre les dromadaires avec les chameaux, j'attire, mesdames, messieurs et chers dromadaires, votre attention sur ce fait: le chameau a deux bosses, mais le dromadaire n'en a qu'une! »

Tous les gens de la salle disaient: « Oh, oh, très intéressant », et les chameaux, les dromadaires, les hommes, les femmes et les enfants prenaient des notes sur leur petit calepin.

THE UNHAPPY DROMEDARY

One day there was a young dromedary who wasn't the least bit happy.

The day before, he had said to his friends: "Tomorrow I'm going to a lecture with my father and mother. So there!"

And the others had said: "Oh, oh! He's going to a lecture, isn't that something!" And he was so impatient that he didn't sleep a wink, but it turned out that he was very unhappy because the lecture wasn't at all what he had imagined: there was no music, and he was very disappointed, and he was bored as could be, and felt like crying.

For an hour and three-quarters a big fat monsieur had been talking. In front of the big fat monsieur there was a water pitcher and a denture glass, but with no toothbrush, and from time to time he poured some water into the glass but never once washed his teeth. He was obviously very upset and he was talking about something else, about dromedaries and camels, to be precise.

The young dromedary couldn't stand the heat, and besides, his hump was bothering him, it was rubbing against the back of the chair.

He was very uncomfortable and kept fidgeting in his seat.

Then his mother said to him: "Sit still and let the nice man talk," and she would give his hump a pinch. The young dromedary felt more and more like crying, and he wanted to leave…

Every five minutes the lecturer would repeat: "You especially mustn't confuse dromedaries and camels, and I would call this fact to your attention, mesdames, messieurs, and all you dear dromedaries among us: the camel has two humps and the dromedary has but one!"

Everyone in the hall observed: "My my! How interesting!" and the camels, the dromedaries, the men, women, and children took notes on little pads.

Et puis le conférencier recommençait: « Ce qui différencie les deux animaux, c'est que le dromadaire n'a qu'une bosse, tandis que, chose étrange et utile à savoir, le chameau en a deux… »

À la fin, le jeune dromadaire en eut assez et se précipitant sur l'estrade, il mordit le conférencier:

« Chameau! » dit le conférencier furieux.

Et tout le monde dans la salle criait: « Chameau, sale chameau, sale chameau! »

Pourtant c'était un dromadaire, et il était très propre.

And the lecturer would start up again: "Yes. What distinguishes the two animals is the fact that the dromedary has only one hump, whereas—most curious and most useful detail—the camel has two…"

Finally the young dromedary had had quite enough, and, jumping onto the platform, he gave the lecturer a healthy bite.

"F-filthy c-ca…" sputtered the lecturer, in a rage. "F-filthy c-ca… c-camel… c-ca… c-ca…," he thundered.[1]

And everyone in the hall repeated: "Camel caca!… Camel caca!"

But the youngster was, to be sure, a dromedary.

And quite a clean one at that.

---

[1] Prévert's untranslatable conclusion plays, of course, on the common insult "*sale chameau*" (dirty camel) where English would say something like "filthy swine." My somewhat baroque rendition attempts to convey its pejorative nature and its literal misinterpretation.

L'ÉLÉPHANT DE MER

Celui-là, c'est l'éléphant de mer, mais il n'en sait rien. L'éléphant de mer ou l'escargot de Bourgogne, ça n'a pas de sens pour lui, il se moque de ces choses-là, il ne tient pas à être quelqu'un.

Il est assis sur le ventre parce qu'il se trouve bien assis comme ça: chacun a le droit de s'asseoir à sa guise.

Il est très content parce que le gardien lui donne des poissons, des poissons vivants.

Chaque jour, il mange des kilos et des kilos de poissons vivants. C'est embêtant pour les poissons vivants parce qu'après ça ils sont morts, mais chacun a le droit de manger à sa guise.

Il les mange sans faire de manières, très vite, tandis que l'homme quand il mange une truite, il la jette d'abord dans l'eau bouillante et, après l'avoir mangée, il en parle encore pendant des jours, des jours et des années:

« Ah! Quelle truite, mon cher, vous vous souvenez! » etc.

Lui, l'éléphant de mer, mange simplement. Il a un très bon petit œil, mais quand il est en colère, son nez en forme de trompe se dilate et ça fait peur à tout le monde.

Son gardien ne lui fait pas de mal... On ne sait jamais ce qui peut arriver... Si tous les animaux se fâchaient, ce serait une drôle d'histoire. Vous voyez ça d'ici, mes petits amis, l'armée des éléphants de terre et de mer arrivant à Paris. Quel gâchis...

L'éléphant de mer ne sait rien faire d'autre que de manger du poisson, mais c'est une chose qu'il fait très bien. Autrefois, il y avait, paraît-il, des éléphants de mer qui jonglaient avec des armoires à glace, mais on ne peut pas savoir si c'est vrai... Personne ne veut plus prêter son armoire!

L'armoire pourrait tomber, la glace pourrait se casser, ça ferait des frais; l'homme aime bien les animaux mais il tient davantage à ses meubles...

THE ELEPHANT SEAL

That one over there is the elephant seal, some call him the sea elephant but it's all the same to him. Elephant seal or Burgundy snail, he couldn't care less. He's not anxious to be a somebody.

He's sitting on his belly because he's comfortable sitting like that: everyone has the right to sit the way they like.

He's very happy because the keeper is throwing him fish, live fish.

Each day he eats loads and loads of live fish. It's not very pleasant for the live fish because after that they're dead, but everyone has the right to eat the way they like.

He eats them without a fuss, very fast, not like a man when he eats a trout, and first he throws it into the boiling water and, after he eats it, he talks and talks about it, for days and days, years even:

"Ah! What a trout, my friend, something to remember!" etc. etc.

Not like the sea elephant. He eats very simply. He has a keen little eye, but when he gets angry his snout, like a trunk, begins to spread out, wider and wider, and everybody gets frightened.

His keeper never does anything at all to hurt him… You never know what might happen… If all the animals got angry it would be quite the affair. You can just imagine, my little friends, the army of land elephants and sea elephants all of a sudden marching on Paris. What a mess…

The only thing the sea elephant knows how to do is eat fish, but it's something he does very well.

Once upon a time, it seems, there were elephant seals who used to juggle with mirrored vanity tables, but there's no way of knowing if it's true or not. Nowadays nobody wants to lend them one.

It could fall, the mirror could smash, and that would be an expense. People like animals but they're more attached to their furniture.

L'éléphant de mer, quand on ne l'ennuie pas, est heureux comme un roi, beaucoup plus heureux qu'un roi, parce qu'il peut s'asseoir sur le ventre quand ça lui fait plaisir alors que le roi, même sur le trône, est toujours assis sur son derrière.

As long as you don't disturb him, the elephant seal is happy as a king, happier than a king in fact because he can sit on his belly when the mood hits him, and the king, even on a throne, always has to sit on his behind.

---

[1] The *"petits amis"* are the young readers for whom Prévert wrote this, the following, and the two preceding prose poems taken from a group of eight entitled *"Contes pour enfants pas sages"* (Tales for naughty children). See page 41, note 1.

CHEVAL DANS UNE ÎLE

Celui-là, c'est le cheval qui vit tout seul quelque part très loin dans une île.

Il mange un peu d'herbe; derrière lui, il y a un bateau; c'est le bateau sur lequel le cheval est venu, c'est le bateau sur lequel il va repartir.

Ce n'est pas un cheval solitaire, il aime beaucoup la compagnie des autres chevaux; tout seul, il s'ennuie, il voudrait faire quelque chose, être utile aux autres. Il continue à manger de l'herbe et pendant qu'il mange, il pense à son grand projet.

Son grand projet, c'est de retourner chez les chevaux pour leur dire:

—Il faut que cela change.

Et les chevaux demanderont:

—Qu'est-ce qui doit changer?

Et lui, il répondra:

—C'est notre vie qui doit changer, elle est trop misérable, nous sommes trop malheureux, cela ne peut pas durer.

Mais les plus gros chevaux, les mieux nourris, ceux qui traînent les corbillards des grands de ce monde, les carrosses des rois et qui portent sur la tête un grand chapeau de paille de riz, voudront l'empêcher de parler et lui diront:

—De quoi te plains-tu, cheval, n'es-tu pas la plus noble conquête de l'homme?

Et ils se moqueront de lui.

Alors tous les autres chevaux, les pauvres traîneurs de camion n'oseront pas donner leur avis.

Mais lui, le cheval qui réfléchit dans l'île, il élèvera la voix:

—S'il est vrai que je suis la plus noble conquête de l'homme, je ne veux pas être en reste avec lui.

« L'homme nous a comblés de cadeaux, mais l'homme a été trop généreux avec nous, l'homme nous a donné le fouet, l'homme nous

HORSE ON AN ISLAND

That one, over there, is the horse, who lives all alone, way off, somewhere on an island.

He's eating a little grass. Behind him there's a boat; it's the boat he came in on, it's the boat that he'll leave on too.

He's not a horse who likes being alone; he loves to be with other horses. All alone he gets bored. He would like to do something, to be useful to others. He keeps eating his grass and, while he eats, he mulls over his big plan.

His big plan is to go back to where the horses live and to tell them:

"This has got to change."

And the horses will ask:

"What's got to change?"

And he'll answer:

"Our life. It's got to change. It's too miserable, and we're too unhappy. It can't go on like this."

But the biggest of the horses, the best fed among them, the ones who pull the hearses of this world's great men, the carriages of kings, and who sport on their heads nice big straw hats, will try to shut him up, and they'll say: "What's your problem, horse? Aren't you the most noble conquest of man?"

And they'll tease him and make fun.

Then all the other horses, the poor cart-and-wagon drudges, won't dare speak their mind.

But this one, the horse who is mulling his plan on the island, will raise his voice:

"If it's true that I'm the most noble conquest of man, I don't want to be obliged or fail to pay him back!

"Man has showered us with gifts. He's been too generous with us. He's given us the whip; he's given us the crop, and spurs, and

a donné la cravache, les éperons, les œillères, les brancards, il nous a
mis du fer dans la bouche et du fer sous les pieds, c'était froid, mais
il nous a marqués au fer rouge pour nous réchauffer...

« Pour moi, c'est fini, il peut reprendre ses bijoux, qu'en pensez-
vous? Et pourquoi a-t-il écrit sérieusement et en grosses lettres sur
les murs... sur les murs de ses écuries, sur les murs de ses casernes
de cavalerie, sur les murs de ses abattoirs, de ses hippodromes et de
ses boucheries hippophagiques: « Soyez bons pour les Animaux? »
Avouez tout de même que c'est se moquer du monde des chevaux!

« Alors, tous les autres pauvres chevaux commenceront à com-
prendre et tous ensemble ils s'en iront trouver les hommes et ils leur
parleront très fort. »

LES CHEVAUX

Messieurs, nous voulons bien traîner vos voitures, vos charrues,
faire vos courses et tout le travail, mais reconnaissons que c'est un
service que nous vous rendons: il faut nous en rendre aussi. Souvent,
vous nous mangez quand nous sommes morts, il n'y a rien à dire là-
dessus, si vous aimez ça; c'est comme pour le petit déjeuner du matin,
il y en a qui prennent de l'avoine au café au lit, d'autres de l'avoine
au chocolat, chacun ses goûts; mais souvent aussi, vous nous frappez:
cela, ça ne doit plus se reproduire.

De plus, nous voulons de l'avoine tous les jours; de l'eau fraîche
tous les jours et puis des vacances et qu'on nous respecte, nous
sommes des chevaux, on n'est pas des bœufs.

Premier qui nous tape dessus, on le mord.

Deuxième qui nous tape dessus, on le tue. Voilà.

Et les hommes comprendront qu'ils ont été un peu fort, ils de-
viendront plus raisonnables.

Il rit, le cheval, en pensant à toutes ces choses qui arriveront sûre-
ment un jour.

Il a envie de chanter, mais il est tout seul, et il n'aime que chanter
en chœur; alors il crie tout de même: « Vive la liberté! »

blinders, and shafts to tug the wagons between. And he put iron in our jaws and iron beneath our feet. And it was cold, but he branded us with red-hot pokers, just to keep us warm…

"Me? I've had enough. He can take back his trinkets, don't you think? And why has he written on the walls, in big, bold letters… On the walls of his stables, on the walls of his cavalry barracks, on the walls of his slaughter-houses, of his hippodromes and his horse-flesh butcher shops. Why has he written: 'Be kind to animals'? You've got to admit, it's a slap in the horse world's face!"

Then all the other poor horses will begin to understand, and they'll go off together looking for men, and when they find them they'll speak out to them, good and loud:

THE HORSES

Messieurs, we're quite willing to pull your plows, to run your errands, and do all the work. But let us state here and now that we do so as a service, and that you owe us one in return. Often you eat us when we're dead, and we have no objection if that's your pleasure. Like with breakfast: some café-au-layabeds[1] take their coffee and oats lying down, some feel their oats with chocolate. To each his own. But you often beat us too, and that simply has got to stop.

Besides, we want our oats every day, and fresh water every day, and vacations too. And we want to be respected. We're horses, after all, not oxen.

The first one to hit us, we bite.

The second one to hit us, we kill. That's that.

And the men will understand that they've gone a little too far, and they'll become more reasonable.

And our horse laughs, thinking of all the things that are bound to happen one day.

He feels like singing, but he's all alone and he really doesn't like to sing by himself. But he cries out all the same: "Vive la liberté!"

Dans d'autres îles, d'autres chevaux l'entendent et ils crient à leur tour de toutes leurs forces: « Vive la liberté! »

Tous les hommes des îles et ceux du continent entendent des cris et se demandent ce que c'est, puis ils se rassurent et disent en haussant les épaules: « Ce n'est rien, c'est des chevaux. »

Mais ils ne se doutent pas de ce que les chevaux leur préparent.

Other horses on other islands hear him, and they cry out too, loud as they can: "Vive la liberté!"

All the men on the islands, and the ones on the continent, hear cries and wonder what ever can they mean. But reassured, they shrug their shoulders and tell one another:

"It's nothing. It's just horses."

And they have no idea what the horses have in store.

---

[1] Knowing Prévert, I believe that the original *"café au lit"* is not a misprint but is intended as a pun on *"café au lait,"* and treat it accordingly.

LES PREMIERS ÂNES

Autrefois, les ânes étaient tout à fait sauvages, c'est-à-dire qu'ils mangeaient quand ils avaient faim, qu'ils buvaient quand ils avaient soif et qu'ils couraient dans l'herbe quand ça leur faisait plaisir.

Quelquefois, un lion venait qui mangeait un âne; alors tous les autres ânes se sauvaient en criant comme des ânes, mais le lendemain ils n'y pensaient plus et recommençaient à braire, à boire, à manger, à courir, à dormir En somme, sauf les jours où le lion venait, tout marchait assez bien.

Un jour, les rois de la création (c'est comme ça que les hommes aiment à s'appeler entre eux) arrivèrent dans le pays des ânes et les ânes, très contents de voir du nouveau monde, galopèrent à la rencontre des hommes.

LES ÂNES
(Ils parlent en galopant)

Ce sont de drôles d'animaux blêmes, ils marchent à deux pattes, leurs oreilles sont très petites, ils ne sont pas beaux, mais il faut tout de même leur faire une petite réception... c'est la moindre des choses...

Et les ânes font les drôles, ils se roulent dans l'herbe en agitant les pattes, ils chantent la chanson des ânes et puis, histoire de rire, ils poussent les hommes pour les faire un tout petit peu tomber par terre; mais l'homme n'aime pas beaucoup la plaisanterie quand ce n'est pas lui qui plaisante, et il n'y a pas cinq minutes que les rois de la création sont dans le pays des ânes que tous les ânes sont ficelés comme des saucissons.

Tous, sauf le plus jeune, le plus tendre, celui-là mis à mort et rôti à la broche avec autour de lui les hommes, le couteau à la main. L'âne cuit à point, les hommes commencent à manger et font une grimace de mauvaise humeur, puis jettent leur couteau par terre.

THE FIRST ASSES

Time was when asses were not civilized in the slightest, that is, they would eat when they were hungry, drink when they were thirsty, and go running about in the grass when the spirit moved them.

Sometimes a lion would come and eat an ass; then all the other asses would run off, crying ass-like cries, but the next day they would forget all about it and start once again to bray, and drink, and eat, and run, and sleep... In short, except for the days when the lion would show up, things were quite orderly and worked out nicely.

One day, the kings of creation—that's the name men take when they're talking amongst themselves—arrived in ass country, and the asses, pleased to see new folks, went galloping to greet them.

THE ASSES
(Speaking as they gallop)

They certainly are odd-looking, these animals. And so pale... And they walk on two paws, their ears are very small, they're not very pretty. But still, we should have a little welcome party for them. It's the very least, after all...

So the asses cavort about, ass-like, roll around on the grass, wag their hooves, sing their ass song, and then, for fun, they up and give the men a friendly shove to push them down on the ground just a little. But man doesn't much care for jokes when he's not the joker, and the kings of creation haven't been in ass country for five minutes when all the asses are tied round and strung up like sausages.

All of them, except the youngest and tenderest one, that is. He's killed and roasted on a spit as the men stand about with knives in hand. When the ass is quite done, the men begin eating, grimacing in disgust and throwing down their knives.

L'UN DES HOMMES
(Il parle tout seul)

Ça ne vaut pas le bœuf, ça ne vaut pas le bœuf!

UN AUTRE

Ce n'est pas bon, j'aime mieux le mouton!

UN AUTRE

Oh que c'est mauvais! (Il pleure).

Et les ânes captifs, voyant pleurer l'homme, pensent que c'est le remords qui lui tire les larmes.

« On va nous laisser partir », pensent les ânes; mais les hommes se lèvent et parlent tous ensemble en faisant de grands gestes.

CHŒUR DES HOMMES

Ces animaux ne sont pas bons à manger, leurs cris sont désagréables, leurs oreilles ridiculement longues, ils sont sûrement stupides et ne savent ni lire, ni compter, nous les appellerons des ânes parce que tel est notre bon plaisir et ils porteront nos paquets. C'est nous qui sommes les rois, en avant!

Et les hommes emmenèrent les ânes.

ONE OF THE MEN
(Speaking alone.)

It's certainly not steak! It's certainly not steak!

ANOTHER

It's awful! I'll take mutton!

ANOTHER

Oh! It's foul! (He starts to cry.)

And the captive asses, seeing the man cry, think that it's remorse that is making him shed his tears.

"They're going to let us go," the asses say to themselves. But the men stand up and all begin to talk at once, waving their arms around.

CHORUS OF THE MEN

These animals are no good to eat, their voices are unpleasant, their ears are absurdly long, they certainly must be stupid, they can't read or count, so we'll call them asses because that's our pleasure, and they'll carry our loads. We're the kings. Forward, march!

And the men went off, dragging their asses behind them.[1]

---

[1] I apologize to the author's shades for not having the good taste to resist, in my translation, a pun that the reader will note is not in the original.

ET DIEU CHASSA ADAM...

Et Dieu chassa Adam à coups de canne à sucre
Et ce fut le premier rhum sur la terre

Et Adam et Ève trébuchèrent
dans les vignes du Seigneur
la sainte Trinité les traquait
mais ils s'obstinaient à chanter
d'une enfantine voix d'alphabet
Dieu et Dieu quatre
Dieu et Dieu quatre
Et la sainte Trinité pleurait
Sur le triangle isocèle et sacré
un biangle isopoivre brillait
et l'éclipsait.

AND GOD CAST ADAM OUT...

And God cast Adam out smote him with sugar cane
And Adam first tasted rum, said "Ah, damn!"[1]

Adam and Eve were overcome
and stumbled through the vineyards of the Lord
the holy Trinity went following
but all the two would do was sing
a childish alphabetic song humdrum
God and God two what four
God and God two what four
And the holy Trinity wept whining—
sacred isosceles—as a newfangled
hotsauceles eclipsing it two-angled[2]
kept it from shining.

---

[1] The original plays, typically, on the identical sound of *premier rhum* (first rum) and *premier homme* (first man).

[2] If the slightly irreverent play on the French *deux et deux quatre* (two and two [make] four) is evident in my attempted translation, the same can probably not be said for my "hotsauceles," an effort to suggest Prévert's *isopoivre*, which itself plays on the usual coupling of *poivre* (pepper) and *sel* (salt), the latter homophonic with *isocèle.*

DES PREMIERS PARENTS...

Caïn et Abel avaient une sœur unique qu'ils
appelaient Putain et Rebelle.
Un beau jour ils s'entre-tuèrent pour elle.
—Ça commence bien, dit Adam.
—Tu trouves? dit Ève en souriant.
—Enfin, tout de même, tu avoueras que c'est tragique!
dit Adam.
—La tragédie, ce n'est pas grand-chose, dit Ève.
Une absence de savoir-vivre.

Et elle se reprit à rêver.
De temps à autre le serpent, en bon petit chien bien élevé, lui
apportait la pomme que parfois Ève daignait lui lancer.

OF THE FIRST PARENTS...

Cain and Abel had an only sister and they
called her Rebel and Whore.
One fine day they killed each other over her.
Only her, nothing more.
"I'd say we're off to a great start, Madam,"
said Adam.
Said Eve with a smile: "You think so, monsieur?"
Said Adam: "Well, anyway, you've got to believe it's tragic!"
"Oh?" answered Eve.
"Tragedy is no big deal, in fact.
Just a lack of tact."

And again she lapsed into introspection.
The serpent like a nice little well-bred dog would bring
the apple now and then, which Eve would deign to fling
in Adam's direction.[1]

---

[1] Though the grammar is ambiguous, it seems clear from the context that the *"lui"*
(to him) to whom Eve would throw the apple was Adam and not the serpent.

OPÉRA TONIQUE

À Isidore Ducasse

Poulpe, oh, regarde-moi! dit l'homme devant son miroir en
balançant les bras, en agitant les mains, en frissonnant
des doigts.
Poulpe au regard de soi, l'homme-pieuvre dans la glace apparaît
et ses tentacules roses, blêmes et frémissants, font des signes
de croix endiablés.
Le miroir est un aquarium où l'homme-pieuvre s'est enfermé.

L'aquarium, est emporté par la grande marée.
L'homme-pieuvre découvre avec terreur les balayeurs de la mer
qui le rejettent sur la terre avec les derniers déchets atom-
iques mêlés aux os de Trafalgar, de Pearl Harbour, du Titanic.

Dansent et chantent alors les sirènes de chair et d'eau, les
hommes-grenouilles et les hommes-cachalots.
Et c'est un opéra de la plus belle eau comique..

TONIC OPERA

for Isidore Ducasse[1]

"Octopus, look! Oh, look at me!" cries the man before the mirror,
   arms flailing, hands waving, his fingers shivering.
Octopod silk-glaze self-gaze[2], the octopus-man appears in the
   glass, and his tentacles, pink, and pale, and quivering, make
   devilishly feverish signs of the cross.
The glass is an aquarium enclosing the octopus-man inside.

The aquarium is carried away in the tide.
The octopus-man is terrified to find the sea-sweepers whisking
   him to the land with the last atomic wastes mixed together
   with the bones from Trafalgar, Pearl Harbor, the Titanic.

Then the mermaids of flesh and water sing and dance, so many
   frog-and-whale-man celebrants.
And it's an opera, high-watermark of comedy oceanic.

---

[1] Isidore Ducasse, alias le comte de Lautréamont (1846–1870), was the author of
the long surrealist prose poem, *Les Chants de Maldoror*, published posthumously in
1870, much admired by Prévert.

[2] To suggest something of the original I make explicit with rhyme and alliteration
Prévert's play on *"soi"* (self) and *"soie"* (silk), implicit in Lautréamont's hallucinatory
apostrophe to the sea, *"Poulpe au regard de soie"* (Octopus with the silken gaze),
from canto 1, section 9.

ACTUALITÉS

À New York ou ailleurs, assis dans son fauteuil de gloire, Lindbergh, l'aviateur, peut voir—comme si c'était lui—l'acteur qui joue le rôle qu'il a lui-même joué dans l'histoire.

Au cinéma du Moulin Rouge, aujourd'hui, par la porte entrouverte de la cabine de l'opérateur, on perçoit des clameurs, celles de la foule des porteurs en triomphe, à l'atterrissage au Bourget en 1927.

Ailleurs encore, dans une cinémathèque, Védrines atterrit en 1919 sur le toit des Galeries Lafayette.

Mais en même temps dehors, c'est-à-dire aujourd'hui encore à Paris, le ciel du dimanche craque dans la tête des gens.

Festival au Bourget.

Comme jeu de cartes au cirque par deux mains tenaces et crispées, la tendre lumière du printemps est déchirée, jetée, éparpillée.

Les monte-en-l'air, les perceurs de muraille, les creveurs de plafond font leur exhibition.

Sabres et scies et bistouris stridents.

La fraise du dentiste singe le chant du grillon et de pauvres rats volants en combinaison Frankenstein foncent à toute vitesse vers la ratière du temps.

Malheureux vagabonds.

Terrain vague du ciel et palissade du son.

L'écran des actualités toujours et de plus en plus bordé de noir est une obsédante lettre de faire part où ponctuellement, hebdomadairement, Zorro, Tarzan et Robin des Bois sont terrassés par le millepattes atomique.

Pourtant, au studio, sur leurs passerelles, écrasés de lumière, les travailleurs du film, comme sur leurs bateaux les travailleurs de la mer, poursuivent leur labeur.

NEWSREEL

In New York or wherever, sitting in his glory seat, Lindbergh, the aviator, is able to see—as if he were the very one—the actor portraying the role he himself played in history.

At the Cinéma du Moulin Rouge, today, through the door of the projectionist's booth, slightly ajar, one can hear the clamor, the cheers of those bearing in triumph the hero who landed at Le Bourget in 1927.

Elsewhere, in a film library, Védrines is landing in 1919 on the roof of the Galeries Lafayette.[1]

But at the same time, today that is, outside and still in Paris, the Sunday sky crackles in the people's heads.

Festival at Le Bourget.

Like a deck of cards in a circus act, gripped in two tight-clenched fists, spring's tender light is ripped, flung, scattered.

The cat-burglars, the second-story men, the break-in artists are exhibiting their talents.

Sabres' and saws' and strident scalpels' blare.

The dentist drill apes the song of the cricket and poor flying rats in Frankenstein smock go hurtling toward time's rat-hole lair.

Poor wretches wandering round.

Vacant lot of sky and picket fence of sound.

Still the newsreel screen edged more and more in black is a hounding, haunting announcement where promptly, time after time, week after week, Zorro, Tarzan, and Robin Hood are laid low by the atomic centipede.

Meanwhile, in the studio, on their walkways and gangplanks beneath light's crushing weight, toilers of the film, like the toilers of the sea in their ships, perform their labors.

Et la ville, en extérieurs, poursuit comme eux le film de sa vie, le film
de Paris.

Le long des quais, la Seine est calme comme un lit bien fait.

Signe de vie verte, un brin d'herbe surgit entre deux pavés.

Une fille s'arrête et respire.

—Oh! je respire, oui je respire et cela me fait autant plaisir que de
fumer une cigarette. J'avais oublié que je respirais. C'est mer-
veilleux, l'air de la vie n'est pas encore tout à fait empoisonné!

Elle sourit, la joie est dans ses yeux, la joie oubliée, retrouvée et
remerciée.

Un garçon s'approche d'elle et lui demande de l'air, comme on de-
mande du feu.

Le ciel recommence à grincer, mais le couple s'embrasse, l'herbe rare
frémit, le film continue, le film de l'amour, le film de la vie.

And the city, with its outdoor shots, performs like them the film of
its life, the film of Paris.
Along its embankments, the Seine is as calm as a well-made bed.
Sign of green life, a blade of grass pokes up between two paving
stones.
A young girl stops to take a breath.
"Oh! I can breathe. Yes, I can really breathe. And it feels as good as
smoking a cigarette. I'd forgotten that I could breathe. It's won-
derful. The air of life hasn't all been poisoned yet!"
She smiles, with joy in her eyes, a joy forgotten, now found again,
and felt with thanks.
A young man walks up to her and asks her for some air, as if asking
for a light.
The sky begins to creak, but the couple kisses, the sparse grass quiv-
ers, the film goes on, the film of love, the film of life.

---

[1] Early aviation hero and World War I pilot Jules Védrines, born in 1881, actually
did land his light plane on the roof of the Parisian department store on January
19, 1919. Hungry for publicity after the war, he performed his feat for the sum of
25,000 francs, much to the displeasure of city authorities. He died three months
later in a crash on a Paris–Rome mail run that he had established.

VOYAGES

Moi aussi
comme les peintres
j'ai mes modèles

Un jour
et c'est déjà hier
sur la plate-forme de l'autobus
je regardais les femmes
qui descendaient la rue d'Amsterdam
Soudain à travers la vitre du bus
j'en découvris une
que je n'avais pas vue monter
Assise et seule elle semblait sourire
À l'instant même elle me plut énormément
mais au même instant
je m'aperçus que c'était la mienne
J'étais content.

TRAVELS

Me too
like painters
I have my models

One day
it was just yesterday
on the platform of the bus
I watched the women
walking down Rue d'Amsterdam
Suddenly through the window of the bus
there was one I noticed
one that I hadn't seen get on
Sitting alone she seemed to be smiling
Just at that very moment exact
she pleased me mightily
but then I had
a revelation... she
was mine in fact
And I was glad.

SPECTACLE
(1949)

ÉTEIGNEZ LES LUMIÈRES

Deux hirondelles dans la lumière
au-dessus de la porte et debout dans leur nid
remuent à peine la tête
en écoutant la nuit
Et la nuit est toute blanche
Et la lune noire de monde
grouillante de sélénites
Un bonhomme de neige
affolé
frappe à la porte de cette lune
Éteignez les lumières
deux amants font l'amour
sur la place des Victoires
Éteignez les lumières.
ou le monde va les voir
Je marchais au hasard
je suis tombé sur eux
elle a baissé sa jupe
il a fermé les yeux
mais ses deux yeux à elle
c'étaient deux pierres à feu

Deux hirondelles dans la lumière
au-dessus de leur porte et debout dans leur nid
remuent à peine la tête
en écoutant la nuit.

TURN OFF YOUR LIGHT

Two swallows in the light
over the doorway standing in their nest
scarcely turn their heads
just listening to the night
And the night is all white
And the moon is a-bustle
covered black with people
its many a lunarite
A snowman
frantically
knocks at moon's door
Turn off your light
two lovers are making love
on the Place des Victoires
Turn off your light
or people will see them
I was just walking past
and I stumbled across them
she pulled down her skirt
he shut his eyes fast
but hers were two flintstones
afire glowing bright

Two swallows in the light
over the doorway standing in their nest
scarcely turn their heads
just listening to the night.

LA GUERRE

Vous déboisez
imbéciles
vous déboisez
Tous les jeunes arbres avec la vieille hache
vous les enlevez
Vous déboisez
imbéciles
vous déboisez
Et les vieux arbres avec leurs vieilles racines
leurs vieux dentiers
vous les gardez
Et vous accrochez une pancarte
Arbres du bien et du mal
Arbres de la Victoire
Arbres de la Liberté
Et la forêt déserte pue le vieux bois crevé
et les oiseaux s'en vont
et vous restez là à chanter
Vous restez là
imbéciles
à chanter et à défiler.

WAR

You strip the woods
damn fool maniacs
you strip the woods
All the young trees with your age-old axe
you hack and rip down
You strip the woods
damn fool maniacs
you strip the woods
And the old trees with their age-old roots
their old false teeth
those you let stand
And you hang signs on them
Trees of Evil Trees of Good[1]
Trees of Victory
Trees of Liberty
And the forest bare reeks of rotting old wood
and off the birds go winging
and you stay there
damn fool maniacs
You stay there
just parading and singing.

---

[1] Contrary to my usual principle of respecting Prévert's punctuation or lack of it, I take the liberty here of capitalizing two nouns that, like the two following, seem to demand it.

POUR RIRE EN SOCIÉTÉ

Le dompteur a mis sa tête
dans la gueule du lion
moi
j'ai mis seulement deux doigts
dans le gosier du Beau Monde
Et il n'a pas eu le temps
de me mordre
Tout simplement
il a vomi en hurlant
un peu de cette bile d'or
à laquelle il tient tant
Pour réussir ce tour
utile et amusant
Se laver les doigts
soigneusement
dans une pinte de bon sang

Chacun son cirque.

HOW TO LAUGH IN SOCIETY

The trainer stuck his head
into the lion's mouth
me
I only put two fingers
down High Society's gullet
And it didn't have time
to bite at me
All it did
was to puke out noisily
a bit of that golden bile
it hoards so preciously
To perform this useful
and amusing feat
Carefully
wash your fingers nice and neat
in a flagon of blood[1]
for a bloody good laugh

To each his own circus.

---

[1] Prévert's next-to-last lines recall the expression *"se faire payer une pinte de bon sang"* (treat oneself to a pint of good blood), meaning roughly to have an uproarious time.

SIGNES

Dans ces ruines nul vestige de meubles de pierres de bêtes nulle
trace de souvenir du vent ni feuilles mortes ni eaux mortes pas le
plus petit débris de lampe à pétrole de lampe à souder point de fil
électrique arraché point de lanternes ni de lampions point de sus-
pension
Dans ces ruines on n'entendait aucun souffle aucun bruit aucun
soupir point[1] d'appel point de supplication point d'interrogation
point d'exclamation Il y avait seulement un petit maçon avec un
petit accent tantôt aigu tantôt grave et cela faisait une petite musique
circonflexe et c'était aussi le toit de sa maison.

SIGNS

In these ruins not a vestige of furniture of stones of animals not a trace of remembrance of the wind or of deathly dry leaves or of deathly still water not the slightest little ruin of an oil lamp of a blowtorch not the slightest electric wire ripped free not the slightest lantern of metal of paper not the slightest chandelier
In these ruins could be heard not a breath not a sound not a sigh not the slightest calling the slightest pleading not the slightest question or exclamation the slightest punctuation marked remarked There was only a little mason with a sharp-pointed little accent first acute then grave and it was making its little circumflected music that was at the same time his housetop's pointed roof.

---

[1] These lines are rather convoluted in their wordplay. First, the double meaning of *point,* both a noun, as in *"point d'interrogation"* and *"point d'exclamation,"* and as a negative. Untranslatable, it can only be suggested. Also, anyone with a rudimentary knowledge of French punctuation will recognize the reference to the circumflex accent—at once a written accent and the mason's "pointed" spoken accent— the former composed of an acute and a grave, humorously said to suggest a pointed roof.

PAR LE TEMPS QUI COURT!

Il faudrait trouver l'historien
le sociologue le philosophe le pédagogue le métaphysicien qui
    aurait
logiquement
simplement
scientifiquement
économiquement
vu
prédit
entrevu
ou aperçu

HISTORIQUEMENT

En 1750 ce qui se passerait en 1780
En 1780 ce qui se passerait en 1793
En 1793 ce qui se passerait en 1815
En 1815 ce qui se passerait en 1830
En 1830 ce qui se passerait en 1848
En 1848 ce qui se passerait en 1870
En 1870 ce qui se passerait en 1871
En 1871 ce qui se passerait en 1900
En 1900 ce qui se passerait en 1914
En 1914 ce qui se passerait en 1918
En 1918 ce qui se passerait en 1936
En 1936 ce qui se passerait en 1940
En 1940 ce qui se passerait en 1944
En 1944 ce qui se passerait en 1950
En 1951 ce qui se passera en 1970 et 11

Et ceci simplement concernant une des régions où beaucoup
    parmi nous vivent actuellement.

IN TIMES LIKE THESE!

We must find the historian
the sociologist philosopher pedagogue metaphysician who would
logically
simply
scientifically
economically
have seen
foreseen
foretold
or glimpsed

HISTORICALLY

In 1750 what would happen in 1780
In 1780 what would happen in 1793
In 1793 what would happen in 1815
In 1815 what would happen in 1830
In 1830 what would happen in 1848
In 1848 what would happen in 1870
In 1870 what would happen in 1871
In 1871 what would happen in 1900
In 1900 what would happen in 1914
In 1914 what would happen in 1918
In 1918 what would happen in 1936
In 1936 what would happen in 1940
In 1940 what would happen in 1944
In 1944 what would happen in 1950
In 1951 what would happen in 1970 and 71

And this only concerning one of the regions where many of us
    are currently living.

REPRÉSENTATION

Des représentants de commerce du Peuple sont en scène et échangent de terribles invectives.

Le rideau tombe et se relève sans que les acteurs y aient prêté attention et ils continuent leur « conversation ».

—Qu'est-ce que cela peut faire que je lutte pour la mauvaise cause puisque je suis de bonne foi?

—Et qu'est-ce que ça peut faire que je sois de mauvaise foi puisque c'est pour la bonne cause?

Ils se saluent.

Le rideau tombe puis se relève.
Ils s'en aperçoivent et s'invectivent.

PERFORMANCE

Traveling salesmen of the People are performing on stage, hurling vicious insults at one another.

The curtain comes down and goes up again unnoticed by the actors, who continue their "chat."

"What difference does it make if I'm fighting for the wrong cause since I'm acting in good faith?"[1]

"And what difference does it make if I'm acting in bad faith since it's for the right cause?"

They nod at each other.

The curtain comes down then goes up again.
They notice it and keep hurling insults at one another.

---

[1] By an accident of translation, my "acting" adds a layer of meaning to the original here that Prévert might (or might not) have approved.

SANGUINE

La fermeture éclair a glissé sur tes reins
et tout l'orage heureux de ton corps amoureux
au beau milieu de l'ombre
a éclaté soudain
Et ta robe en tombant sur le parquet ciré
n'a pas fait plus de bruit
qu'une écorce d'orange tombant sur un tapis
Mais sous nos pieds
ses petits boutons de nacre craquaient comme des pépins
Sanguine
joli fruit
la pointe de ton sein
a tracé une nouvelle ligne de chance
dans le creux de ma main
Sanguine
joli fruit

Soleil de nuit.

BLOOD ORANGE

The zipper down your back goes gliding free
and all the passion in your body's storm
hiding deep in the shadows
bursts forth suddenly
And falling down to the wax-glossed floor
your dress makes no more sound no more
noise than an orange peel
hitting a carpet
But here where we stand
we can hear we can feel
its buttons click like little opal pips
Blood orange
lovely fruit
in the palm of my cupped hand
one of your bosom tips
traces my lifeline's destiny new-spun
Blood orange
lovely fruit

The night-sky sun.

IL A TOURNÉ AUTOUR DE MOI

Il a tourné autour de moi
pendant des mois des jours des heures
et il a posé la main sur mon sein
en m'appelant son petit cœur
Et il m'a arraché une promesse
comme on arrache une fleur à la terre
Et il a gardé cette promesse dans sa tête
comme on garde une fleur dans une serre
J'ai oublié ma promesse
et la fleur tout de suite a fané
Et les yeux lui sont sortis de la tête
il m'a regardée de travers
et il m'a injuriée
Un autre est venu qui ne m'a rien demandé
mais il m'a regardée tout entière
Déjà pour lui j'étais nue
de la tête aux pieds
et quand il m'a déshabillée
je me suis laissé faire
Et je ne savais pas qui c'était.

HE HOVERED ABOUT ME

He hovered about me
for months for days for hours
he called me his sweetheart
and fondled my tit
He plucked from me a promise
as one would pluck flowers
He kept it in his head cared for it cherished it
But soon I forgot the promise I had made
soon the flower will fade
it withers and dies
And he sneers at me with staring leering eyes
heaps me with abuse
Another one came with no hullabaloo
asked for nothing at all but looked me through and through
For him head to toe
I was naked already
and when he undressed me there on the bed he
did what he wanted as I slid below him
And I didn't even know him.

CHANSON DES SARDINIÈRES

Tournez tournez
petites filles
tournez autour des fabriques
bientôt vous serez dedans
tournez tournez
filles des pêcheurs
filles des paysans

Les fées qui sont venues
autour de vos berceaux
les fées étaient payées
par les gens du château
elles vous ont dit l'avenir
et il n'était pas beau

Vous vivrez malheureuses
et vous aurez beaucoup d'enfants
beaucoup d'enfants
qui vivront malheureux
et qui auront beaucoup d'enfants
qui vivront malheureux
et qui auront beaucoup d'enfants
beaucoup d'enfants
qui vivront malheureux
et qui auront beaucoup d'enfants
beaucoup d'enfants
beaucoup d'enfants...

THE SARDINE-PACKERS' SONG

Round round little girls
turn round about
the factory
in hardly a minute
they'll trap you in it
turn round and round
again again
daughters of peasants and fishermen

The fairies who would come and stand
about your cradles—fairy band
kept by the chateau dwellers—would
foretell your fortune as they stood
conjuring up your fortune and
alas it wasn't very good

You'll live in misery
and you'll have lots of children too
children who
will live in misery
and who'll have lots of children who
will live in misery
and who'll have lots of children too
children who
will live in misery
and who'll have lots of children too
lots of children
children
children…

Tournez tournez
petites filles
tournez autour des fabriques
bientôt vous serez dedans
tournez tournez
filles des pêcheurs
filles des paysans.

Round round little girls
turn round about
the factory
in hardly a minute
they'll trap you in it
turn round and round
again again
daughters of peasants and fishermen.

LES ENFANTS QUI S'AIMENT

Les enfants qui s'aiment s'embrassent debout
Contre les portes de la nuit
Et les passants qui passent les désignent du doigt
Mais les enfants qui s'aiment
Ne sont là pour personne
Et c'est seulement leur ombre
Qui tremble dans la nuit
Excitant la rage des passants
Leur rage leur mépris leurs rires et leur envie
Les enfants qui s'aiment ne sont là pour personne
Ils sont ailleurs bien plus loin que la nuit
Bien plus haut que le jour
Dans l'éblouissante clarté de leur premier amour.

CHILDREN IN LOVE

Children in love hug and kiss standing up
Against the doors of night
And passers-by pass and point fingers at them
But children in love
Aren't there for the others
And it's only their shadow
That trembles in the night
Inciting the rage of the passers-by
Their rage their disdain their laughter their envy
But children in love aren't there for the others
They're far far away much farther than the night
Much higher than the day
In the shine of their first love's dizzying dazzling light.

DE GRANDS COCHERS...

De grands cochers intègres
et protecteurs des bêtes
sur le siège du carrosse
où leurs fesses sont posées
agitent au bout d'une perche
une carotte pourpre
et les cochers stimulent
les centaures attelés
en poussant de grands cris
Vive la liberté
Et les centaures galopent
éblouis enivrés
route de la révolte
sans jamais s'arrêter.

GREAT COACHMEN...

Great coachmen virtuous
and animal protectors
on the carriage seats
where their butts repose
dangle a crimson carrot
hanging from a stick
and the coachmen urge on
the centaurs in harness
shouting loud cries
Vive la liberté
And the centaurs go galloping
dazzled drunk
road of revolt
never stopping along the way.

LE DERNIER CARRÉ

Un alcoolonel d'infanterie tropicale
frappé d'hémiplégie anale
s'écroule dans le tourniquet aux tickets
bloquant à lui seul
l'entrée de toute une exposition coloniale

Ses dernières paroles
Ils ne passeront pas.

THE ENDGAME

A generalcoholic[1] he
back from the tropics and the infantry
in semi-paralyzed rectal condition
swoons in a ticket turnstile suddenly
blocking the entrance with his ass
to an entire colonial exposition

His final words
They shall not pass.[2]

---

[1] I hope the reader agrees that "generalcoholic" works as well as Prévert's "*alcoolonel*" with no harm to the meaning.

[2] The snide reference is obviously to the famous declaration of General Pétain at the battle of Verdun in 1916.

ON

C'est un mardi vers quatre heures de l'après-midi
au mois de Février
dans une cuisine
il y a une bonne qui vient d'être humiliée
Au fond d'elle-même
quelque chose qui était encore intact
vient d'être abîmé
saccagé
Quelque chose qui était encore vivant
et qui silencieusement riait
Mais
on est entré
on a dit un mot blessant
à propos d'un objet cassé
et la chose qui était encore capable de rire
s'est arrêtée de rire à tout jamais
Et la bonne reste figée
figée devant l'évier
et puis elle se met à trembler
Mais il ne faut pas qu'elle commence à pleurer
Si elle commençait à pleurer
la bonne à tout faire
elle sait bien qu'elle ne pourrait rien faire
pour s'arrêter
Elle porte en elle une si grande misère
elle la porte depuis si longtemps
comme un enfant mort mais tout de même encore
        un petit peu vivant
Elle sait bien
que la première larme versée

THEY

It's a Tuesday about four o'clock
one February afternoon
and in a kitchen
there's a maid who has just been humiliated
Down deep inside her
something that had been intact
has just been cut
sacked devastated
as they deride her
Something that had been alive
that still could laugh a quiet little laugh
But
then they came in
they said a hurtful word
about a broken something-or-other
and after that the thing in her that could
still laugh stopped laughing now for good
And the maid stands transfixed utterly
beside the sink and she
trembles but knows she has to keep
from crying for if she starts to weep
this handymaid
Jeanne-of-all-trades will be
unable quite to stem her tears
The poverty she bears so long so deep
is like a dead child in her breast clinging to life
    the slightest bit
She knows let one tear flow
then comes the flood of all the rest
and that would cause such blustering
that they would fly into a fit

toutes les autres larmes viendraient
et cela ferait un tel vacarme
qu'on ne pourrait le supporter
et qu'on la chasserait
et que cet enfant mourrait tout à fait

Alors elle se tait.

and they would let her go
and that would be the end and it
would finally kill that child still quivering

And so she doesn't say a thing.

SANG ET PLUMES

Alouette du souvenir
c'est ton sang qui coule
et non pas le mien
Alouette du souvenir
j'ai serré mon poing
Alouette du souvenir
oiseau mort joli
tu n'aurais pas dû venir
manger dans ma main
les graines de l'oubli.

BLOOD AND FEATHERS

Lark of memory
it's your blood flowing
and not my own
Lark of memory
I clenched my fist tight
Lark of memory
beautiful bird but dead no less
you ought not have come back to me
to nibble from my open hand
grains of forgetfulness.

NARCISSE

Narcisse se baigne nu
De jolies filles nues viennent le voir
Narcisse sort de l'eau s'approche d'elles
et s'aperçoit qu'il n'est plus tout à fait le même
Quelque chose en lui a changé
Il se caresse de la main
étonné de donner sans le vouloir ni le savoir
comme un jeune cheval entier
les preuves de sa naissante virilité
Et retourne dans l'eau
plus ébloui que gêné
Et regarde les filles
puis
dans l'eau à mi-corps se regarde encore
Et voit
par un phénomène de réfraction
un bâton brisé
Il se noie
déçu enfantinement désespéré.

NARCISSUS

Narcissus bathes naked
Pretty naked maids come to look
Narcissus leaves the water and approaches them
and notices that he is no longer quite the same
Something in him has changed
He strokes himself with his palm
amazed at giving without wishing or knowing why
the proof of his budding manhood
like a complete young stallion
And returns to the water
more awed than disconcerted
and stands gazing at the maids
then
up to his waist in water looks at himself again
And sees
thanks to the phenomenon of refraction
a shaft bending in two
And he drowns himself
in daft despair and childish distraction.

VAINEMENT

Un vieillard hurle à la mort
et traverse le square en poussant un cerceau
Il crie que c'est l'hiver et que tout est fini
que les carottes sont cuites que les dés sont lâchés
et que la messe est dite et que les jeux sont faits
et que la pièce est jouée et le rideau tiré
Vainement
vainement
De bons amis m'appellent qui me détestent bien
de vieux amis obèses me surveillent montre en main
me supplient de comprendre tout ce qu'ils ont compris
Vainement
vainement
De vrais amis sont morts d'un seul coup tout entiers et d'autres
        vivent encore et rient de toutes leurs dents
les autres les appellent et m'appellent en même temps
Vainement
vainement
Les autres qui sont morts déjà de leur vivant
et qui portent le deuil de leurs rêves d'enfants
et ces gens exemplaires corrects et bien élevés
se tuent à vous prédire ce qui va arriver
et la route toute droite le chemin tout tracé
et la statue de sel la patrie en danger
Le moment est venu de se faire une raison
Déjà au fond du square on entend le clairon
le jardin va fermer
le tambour est voilé
Vainement
vainement

Le jardin reste ouvert pour ceux qui l'ont aimé.

IN VAIN

An old man barks bays at the moon
rolling a hoop across a little park
He cries that it's winter and everything's done and gone
the goose is cooked the dice are thrown
the mass is said and the chips are down
the play is over and the curtain drawn
In vain
in vain
Good friends who loathe me cordially
pudgy old friends who watch me watch in hand
call me beg me to understand what they have known
In vain
in vain
True friends dead all at once together and others still living
        grinning toothsomely
the others call to them and call to me
In vain
in vain
Still others who all through their lives lived dead
in mourning for their childhood dreams pell-mell
and those of exemplary bent well bred
struggling to be the ones to spell
for you what fates await
and the highway traced out the road true and straight
statue of salt and threatened fatherland
The time has come to take a stand
The trumpet blares out through the park
the garden closes after dark
muffled the tales the drums would tell
In vain
in vain

The park stays open for those who loved it well.

LA PLUIE ET LE BEAU TEMPS

(1955)

TOUT S'EN ALLAIT...

Il y avait de faibles femmes
et puis des femmes faciles
et des femmes fatales
qui pleuraient hurlaient sanglotaient
devant des hommes de paille
qui flambaient
Des enfants perdus couraient dans des ruines de rues tout blêmes
    de savoir qu'ils ne se retrouveraient jamais plus
Et des chefs de famille
qui ne reconnaissaient plus le plancher du plafond
voletaient d'un étage à l'autre
dans une pluie de paillassons de suspensions de petites cuillers et
    de plumes d'édredon
Tout s'en allait
La ville s'écroulait
grouillait
s'émiettait
en tournant sur elle-même
sans même avoir l'air de bouger
Des cochons noirs aveuglés
dans la soudaine obscurité
d'une porcherie modèle désaffectée
galopaient
La ville s'en allait
suant sang et eau
gaz éclaté
Ceux qui n'avaient rêvé que plaies et bosses
se réveillaient
décapités
ayant perdu peignes et brosses

IT WAS COMING ALL UNDONE...

There were weak women
and easy women
and *femme fatale* women
who were weeping wailing sobbing
before straw men
all going up in flames
Lost children were running round the streets of rubbled ruins
    deathly pale in the knowledge that they would never be
    found
And family fathers
who couldn't tell ceiling from floor anymore
were flitting up and down from storey to storey
in a storm of doormats chandeliers teaspoons a flurry of quilt
    feathers raining galore
It was coming all undone
The city was falling down
falling in a heap
falling to pieces
twisting turning about itself
though it scarcely seemed to budge
Pigs burning black and blinded
in the sudden darkness
of a model piggery now standing useless
scurried about
The city was coming all undone
oozing of blood and sweat
and gas exploding
Those who had dreamt of bumps and bruises
were waking up
decapitated
their combs and brushes gone

et autres petites mondanités
Une noce toute noire morte sur pied
depuis le garçon d'honneur jusqu'aux mariés
gardait un équilibre de cendre figée
devant un photographe
torréfié terrifié
Nouvelles ruines toutes neuves
hommage de guerre
jeux de reconstruction
profits et pertes
bois et charbons
Sur le dernier carré d'une maison ouvrière
une omelette abandonnée
pendait comme un vieux linge
sur une verrière brisée
et dans les miettes d'un vieux lit calciné mêlées à la sciure grise
    d'un buffet volatilisé
la viande humaine faisait corps-grillé avec la viande à manger
Dans les coulisses du progrès
des hommes intègres poursuivaient intégralement la désintégra-
    tion progressive de la matière vivante
désemparée.

and other such trifles
A wedding party frozen dead in its tracks
stood black stalk-still
in a delicate ashen balance
from the best man to the bride and groom
before a photographer
terrified torrefied
New ruins utterly unknown before
homage to war
reconstruction projects
profits and losses
coal and wood...
On the last patch left standing in a workingman's house
an omelette uneaten
hung like yesterday's tattered wash
on a skylight in shatters
and amid the cinders of an old bed burned to ashes and mixed
    with the gray sawdust of a volatilized buffet
human flesh and sizzling dinner meat lay intertwined as one
In progress's backstage wings
those still intact tactfully pursued the progressive tactual
    disintegration of the stuff of life
disarmed disabled.

SCEAUX D'HOMMES ÉGAUX MORTS

Sur les fesses du chef décapité était tatoué le prénom
    du soldat familier
et le prénom du chef était tatoué sur la poitrine de son
    homme fusillé
Leurs mains enlacées et crispées faisaient semblant de
    vivre encore
Misogynie mère des guerres
Tasses et théières
Seaux d'eau
Mégots morts
Deux corps sous les décombres
dans l'ombre du décor.

SODOMINION'S MINIONS MILITARY

The headless chief's rump was tattooed with the name
    of his faggot soldier-friend
and the chief's name was tattooed on the chest of his buddy
    gunned down in the kill
Each one with tight-clenched fists enlaced that pretend to
    live life still
Misogyny you mother of war
Swish restroom tea-parties
Fawning fauna and flora
Sodominions' Gomorrha
Ifs ands butts galore
Two bodies under the rot's the rubble's
shadowed décor.

---

[1] The reader needs no perspicacity to notice that my title for this tidbit of soldierly homoerotica differs from Prévert's. A little more may be necessary to see why: his, rather meaningless in its entirety ("Men's Seals Dead Equals"), exists merely for the homophone of "Sodome et Gomorrhe." Likewise, lines 6 and 7 of the original, also a semantic stretch ("Pails of water / Dead butts"), necessitate similar translator's license. As for the enigmatic *"tasses et théières"* (cups and teapots), both are used, I suspect, for their slang meaning of public urinal *cum* gay male meetingplace.

L'ORAGE ET L'ÉCLAIRCIE

Un chien fou dans les couloirs d'une maison de santé
cherche son maître mort depuis l'été dernier

Un arbre ou une pendule
un oiseau un couteau
une mauvaise nouvelle
une bonne nouvelle

Ton visage d'enfant
comme une crème terrible
tout à coup s'est figé
Ton sourire
comme une roue dentée
s'est mis à tourner
perdu crispé escamoté
Et l'eau merveilleuse
de tes yeux verts et gris
s'est tarie
La foudre
la petite foudre noire de la haine de la détresse
        et du savoir
a lui
pour moi
Signal de toute la terre
visage en tous sens retourné
message du désespoir
de la lucidité

THE STORM AND THE CLEARING

A mad dog prowling an asylum's halls
looks for its master dead since summer past

A tree or a clock
a bird a knife
a piece of bad news
a piece of good news

Your baby face
like a famous *crème fouettée*
took suddenly firm
Your smile
like a cogged wheel
began to turn
lost-looking tight-lipped cast aside
And your gray-green eyes'
miraculous waters
dried up and died
The thunderbolt
the little black thunderbolt of hate of distress
    of all-knowingness
shone there
for me
Signal world-wide
face everywhere turned inside out
message of despair
of clear-mindedness

Et puis soudain plus rien
rien d'autre que ton visage ingénu enfantin
tout seul comme un volcan éteint

Et puis
la fatigue l'indifférence la gentillesse et l'espoir de dormir
et même le courage de sourire.

And all at once nothing more shone
only your baby-face innocence full-blown
extinct volcano standing alone.

And then
fatigue indifference courteousness and the hope
      to sleep a while
even courage enough to brave a smile.

LA RIVIÈRE

Tes jeunes seins brillaient sous la lune
mais il a jeté
le caillou glacé
la froide pierre de la jalousie
sur le reflet
de ta beauté
qui dansait nue sur la rivière
dans la splendeur de l'été.

THE STREAM

Your young breasts shone beneath the moon
but he has thrown
the icy pebble
the frigid stone of jealousy
on your reflection's
loveliness
dancing naked upon the stream
in summer's splendrous majesty.

LES AMOUREUX TRAHIS

Moi j'avais une lampe
et toi la lumière
Qui a vendu la mèche?

LOVERS BETRAYED

I had an oil lamp[1]
you had the light
who sold the wick and blew the trick?

---

[1] Without specifying an oil lamp the denouement of this briefest of lovers'
breakups—making literal the figurative *"vendre la mèche"* (i.e., "to reveal a se-
cret")—would hardly make sense in English.

QUAND...

Quand le lionceau déjeune
la lionne rajeunit
Quand le feu réclame sa part
la terre rougit
Quand la mort lui parle de l'amour
la vie frémit
Quand la vie lui parle de la mort
l'amour sourit.

WHEN...[1]

When lion cub will slake his hunger
lioness grows younger
When fire demands its due outspread
earth blushes red
When death tells life what love delivers
life duly quivers
When life tells love of death the while
love will just smile.

---

[1] The reader will notice that, beside attempting to explicate this enigmatic poem
a little, I also invoke translator's license by imposing on it a rhyme scheme and
meter rather less casual than Prévert's.

MAINTENANT J'AI GRANDI

Enfant
j'ai vécu drôlement
le fou rire tous les jours
le fou rire vraiment
et puis une tristesse tellement triste
quelquefois les deux en même temps
Alors je me croyais désespéré
Tout simplement je n'avais pas d'espoir
je n'avais rien d'autre que d'être vivant
j'étais intact
j'étais content
et j'étais triste
mais jamais je ne faisais semblant
Je connaissais le geste pour rester vivant
Secouer la tête
pour dire non
secouer la tête
pour ne pas laisser entrer les idées des gens
Secouer la tête pour dire non
et sourire pour dire oui
oui aux choses et aux êtres
aux êtres et aux choses à regarder à caresser
à aimer
à prendre ou à laisser
J'étais comme j'étais
sans mentalité

I'VE GROWN UP NOW

A tot
I lived in a curious way
giggles each and every day
giggles well and true begot
then sadness would weigh sad on me
sometimes both simultaneously
I thought despair was all my lot
It's just that hope was not my destiny
nothing was mine except the fact
of being alive
I was intact
and glad to be
and sad no less
but never would I pretend or act
I knew the gestures to let life continue
Shake your head
to say no
shake your head
lest you let other folks' ideas
settle within you
Shake your head to say no
and smile to say yes
to the things the people
the people and things to gaze at to caress
to love
take it or leave it
That's the way I was
intellectless

Et quand j'avais besoin d'idées
pour me tenir compagnie
je les appelais
Et elles venaient
et je disais oui à celles qui me plaisaient
les autres je les jetais

Maintenant j'ai grandi
les idées aussi
mais ce sont toujours de grandes idées
de belles idées
d'idéales idées
Et je leur ris toujours au nez
Mais elles m'attendent
pour se venger
et me manger
un jour où je serai très fatigué
Mais moi au coin d'un bois
je les attends aussi
et je leur tranche la gorge
je leur coupe l'appétit.

When I needed ideas
to keep me company
I'd call them and some
would come
and I would say
yes if they pleased me and they would stay
the rest I threw away

I've grown up now
the ideas too
but they're still great and grand
lovely ideas
ideal ideas
And I still laugh in their faces yes I do
But there they lie
in wait to take revenge on me
to chew me up
swallow me down
one day when I'm too tired to flee
But here too am I
lying in wait for them to come by
and I'll slit their throat
and I'll snuff out quite
their appetite.

LE TEMPS HALETANT

Émerveillée de tout ne s'étonnant jamais de rien
une fillette chantait
suivant les saisons suivant son chemin

Quand les oignons me feront rire
les carottes me feront pleurer
l'âne de l'alphabet a su m'apprendre à lire
à lire pour de vrai

Mais une manivelle a défait le printemps
et des morceaux de glace lui ont sauté à la figure

J'ai trop de larmes pour pleurer
ils font la guerre à la nature
Moi qui tutoyais le soleil
je n'ose plus le regarder en face.

TIME OUT OF BREATH

In wonder at the world but unamazed
a little girl would sing her song
each season's reasons traveled her along

When onions make me laugh
carrots will make me cry
the ass—A as in ass—taught me to read
and read indeed

But a crank turned round and laid spring low
and chips of ice went flying in her face[1]

I have too many tears to cry
nature and ice are warring now
And though I called the sun by name
I dare no longer look him in the eye.

---

[1] Despite its grammatical masculine gender in French, spring seems feminine to me. (Besides, "in *his* face" would mislead some readers into interpreting "crank" as a person rather than a thing.)

CHANSON POUR VOUS

À Florence

Cheveux noirs cheveux noirs
caressés par les vagues
cheveux noirs cheveux noirs
décoiffés par le vent
Le brouillard de septembre
flotte derrière les arbres
le soleil est un citron vert
Et la Misère
dans sa voiture vide
traînée par trois enfants trop blonds
traverse les décombres
et s'en va vers la mer
Cheveux noirs cheveux noirs
caressés par les vagues
cheveux noirs cheveux noirs
décoiffés par le vent
Avec ses tonneaux de fer
ses débris de ciment armé
comme un chien mort
les pattes en l'air
le radeau de l'Amirauté[1]
gît immobile sur les galets
Cheveux noirs cheveux noirs

SONG FOR YOU

For Florence

Black hair black hair
that the waves caress
black hair black hair
tresses tousled by the breeze
The September fog
hovers behind the trees
the sun is a lime a lemon green
and Poverty
in her empty cart
pulled by three children far too blond
rolls over the debris
and goes yonder to the sea
Black hair black hair
that the waves caress
black hair black hair
tresses tousled by the breeze
And the l'Amirauté raft
pile of junk lying there
fore and aft her iron kegs
each steel-ribbed chunk
like a dog dead on its back
paws up in the air
spread on the flat stones motionless
Black hair black hair

décoiffés par les vagues
cheveux noirs cheveux noirs
caressés par le vent
Soleil
citron vert emporté par le temps
la voix de la sirène
est une voix d'enfant.

tresses tousled by the waves
black hair black hair
that the breeze caresses
Sun
a lime lemon green
carried away by time a-winging
the siren's voice
is a child's voice singing.

---

[1] The reference to *"le radeau de l'Amirauté"* is cryptic at best. I suspect it may be an allusion to the excavation of an 18th-century boat, *le Vengeur*, in the Corsican port of l'Amirauté, but that's only a guess.

L'AMOUR À LA ROBOTE

Un homme écrit à la machine une lettre d'amour et la machine
    répond à l'homme et à la main et à la place de la destinataire
Elle est tellement perfectionnée la machine
la machine à laver les chèques et les lettres d'amour
Et l'homme confortablement installé dans sa machine à habiter lit
    à la machine à lire la réponse de la machine à écrire
Et dans sa machine à rêver avec sa machine à calculer il achète une
    machine à faire l'amour
Et dans sa machine à réaliser les rêves il fait l'amour à la machine
    à écrire à la machine à faire l'amour
Et la machine le trompe avec un machin
un machin à mourir de rire.

AUTO-MATING

A man types a love-letter to the typing-machine[1] and the machine
    writes him an answer in longhand over her address
Machines have been so perfected
the ones that launder checks and love-letters at least[2]
And the man comfortably ensconced in his dwelling-machine
    reads on the reading-machine the typing-machine's reply
And in his dreaming-machine he buys with his spending-machine
    a lovemaking-machine
And in his dreaming-come-true-machine he makes love on the
    lovemaking-machine to the typing-machine
And the typing-machine cheats on him as she proceeds to auto-
    mate
with a machinating something-or-other[3]
funny enough to die for.

---

[1] I realize that "typing-machine" isn't very idiomatic English, but I want to preserve Prévert's typical ambivalence of *"écrit à la machine,"* translatable as both "types" (writes *on* the machine and "writes *to* the machine").

[2] If Prévert allowed himself the luxury of punctuation, I suspect he would put an exclamation mark after this sarcastic and probably parenthetical observation.

[3] No less challenging—impossible?—for the translator is his wordplay on *"machine"* and *"machin,"* which my version can only hint at.

COMME CELA SE TROUVE!

(Ballet)

Le décor représente une maison, un cimetière et un salon de thé.

—Oh, j'ai perdu ma femme! chante et danse le veuf, inconsolable, hilare et désolé, nerfs brisés et raccommodés.

—Mon mari m'a perdue! danse et chante la femme, la morte du vivant, souriante, indifférente, mais toujours aussi triste que dans son temps passé.

—Mon mari m'a perdue, qui jamais ne m'avait trouvée! Il n'a pas de quoi se vanter. Même si c'était lui qui m'avait perdue, aurait-il jamais pu me sauver?

Et ils dansent, du côté cour et du côté jardin, du côté cimetière, du côté salon de thé, ensemble et séparés, ensemble, comme ils dormaient, rêvaient et s'éveillaient, chacun de son mauvais côté.

Et même si la musique est belle, le ballet n'est pas gai.

THE WAY THINGS HAPPEN!

(Ballet)

The set represents a house, a graveyard, and a tearoom.

"Oh! I've lost my wife!" sings and dances the widower, uncon-
    solable, jovial, and distraught, nerves shattered and mended.
"My husband has lost me!" sings and dances the woman, the live
    man's dead wife, smiling, indifferent, but still as sad as in her
    bygone days.
"My husband has lost me, but he had never found me! He has
    nothing to be proud of. Even though he was the one who lost
    me, could he ever have saved me?"
And they dance, stage-leftward, stage-rightward, graveyardward,
    tearoomward, together and apart, together as they had slept,
    and dreamt, and woken up, each on his own her own wrong
    side of the bed.
And even though the music is pretty, the ballet isn't gay.

PETITE TÊTE SANS CERVELLE

C'est un vélo volé et secoué par le vent
un enfant est dessus qui pédale en pleurant
un brave homme derrière lui le poursuit en hurlant
Et le garde-barrière agite son drapeau
l'enfant passe quand même
le train passe sur lui
et le brave homme arrive en reprenant son souffle
contemplant sa ferraille
n'en croyant pas ses yeux
Les deux roues sont tordues
le guidon est faussé
le cadre fracassé
le lampion en charpie
et la bougie en miettes
Et ma médaille de Saint-Christophe
où est-elle passée
vraiment il n'y a plus d'enfants
on ne sait plus à quel saint se vouer
on ne sait plus que dire
on ne sait plus que penser

LITTLE BRAINLESS TOT

A bike taken—stolen—and shaken in the breeze
a tearful tot pedaling hard as you please
a fine monsieur chasing screaming obscenities
And the gate-keeper waving his flag in warning
but the youngster doesn't stop
and he's crushed by the train
and the fine monsieur panting
finally catches up
catches his breath
looks at his pile of junk
can't believe his eyes
The two wheels are bent
the handlebars twisted
the frame pulled askew
the lantern slashed to shreds
the plug smashed to bits
And my Saint-Christopher medal he cries
where the devil is it
really
who knows what these kids will do today
or what saint to pray to
or what to say
or what to think

on ne sait plus comment tout ça va finir
on ne sait plus où on en est
vraiment

Quelle bande de ons
dit le garde-barrière en pleurant.

or how it's going to end
or what's to become of us all or
or really

Bloody bunch of 'ores
cries the gate-keeper weeping.

---

[1] With typical wordplay Prévert sums up the series of "on" in the preceding lines with the clearly suggested obscenity of the exclamation "*bande de ons*" (i.e., bande de *cons*). I follow him in my translation as best I can.

NUAGES

Je suis allée chercher mon tricot de laine et le chevreau m'a suivie
le gris
il ne se méfie pas comme le grand
il est encore trop petit

Elle était toute petite aussi
mais quelque chose en elle parlait déjà vieux comme le monde
Déjà
elle savait des choses atroces
par exemple
qu'il faut se méfier
Et elle regardait le chevreau et le chevreau la regardait
et elle avait envie de pleurer
Il est comme moi
dit-elle
un peu triste et un peu gai
Et puis elle eut un grand sourire
et la pluie se mit à tomber

CLOUDS

She said[1] I went to get my sweater and the goat kid came and
   followed me
the gray one
he's not wary like the big one
he's still too small to be

She was small too no less than he
but something about her already was talking as old as the hills
Already
she knew most unpleasant things
most of all
that you must be wary
And she looked at the kid and the kid looked at her
and she felt like weeping
He's like me
she said
a little sad a little gay
And then she broke out in a great big smile
and the rain started falling

---

[1] I apologize to literalists and purists for my addition of a phrase to introduce the
specifically female poetic voice, asexual in English without it.

SOUVENIR

Vingt ans après cent ans plus tard
toujours les sordides mousquetaires
toujours les mêmes traîneurs de sabre
toujours les porteurs de bannière
Enfant j'ai vu sur une image
des hommes en robe noire avec un visage vert
debout autour d'un homme qui s'appelait Ferrer
Oh pauvres hommes vivants
comme vous avez de redoutables adversaires
toujours les mêmes sans un changement
de malheureux bourreaux
semblables à ceux d'avant.

MEMORY

Twenty years after a hundred years beyond[1]
still the same sordid musketeers
still the same saber-rattling manner
still the same banner-cavaliers
Once as a child I saw a picture where
men in black robes and faces painted green
were seen standing round a man named Ferrer[2]
Oh poor men living your lives now and here
what fearsome foes are yours today to bear
unchanged the same as they once were
wretched executioners
like those of yesteryear.

---

[1] The arithmetic of Prévert's chronology is as unclear in the original as it is in my translation.

[2] I suspect that this vague—to me, at least—allusion may refer to Saint Vincent Ferrer, 15th-century Spanish zealot celebrated for his forceful conversions to Christianity.

À QUOI RÊVAIS-TU?

Vêtue puis revêtue
à quoi rêvais-tu
dévêtue

Je laissais mon vison au vestiaire
et nous partions dans le désert
Nous vivions d'amour et d'eau fraîche
nous nous aimions dans la misère
nous mangions notre linge sale en famine
et sur la nappe de sable noir
tintait la vaisselle du soleil
Nous nous aimions dans la misère
nous vivions d'amour et d'eau fraîche
j'étais ta nue propriété.

WHAT DREAMT YOU OF?

Dressed then re-dressed
my lady-love[1]
undressed
what dreamt you of?

I left my mink in the coatroom attendant's hands
and we went off to roam the desert sands
We lived on love and water cool and fresh
we were in love and poverty
we chewed the scandals of our life and swallowed
our dirty linen famished *en famille*[2]
and on the tablecloth of black sand followed
the clink of empty dishes of the sun
We were in love and poverty
we lived on love and water fresh and cool
I was your naked property.

---

[1] My extra line serves both to establish the gender of the poet's interlocutor, obvious in the French, and to prepare her reply over the rest of the poem.

[2] A little translator's license is necessary here to suggest the wordplay of the expression *"laver son linge sale en famille"* (to wash one's dirty linen in private), while still maintaining the force of the poet's *"famine."*

CONFIDENCES D'UN CONDAMNÉ

Pourquoi on m'a coupé la tête?

Je peux bien le dire maintenant, tout s'efface avec le temps.

C'était si simple, vraiment.

J'étais allé passer la soirée chez des amis mais il y avait beaucoup de monde et je m'ennuyais. À cette époque j'étais un peu triste et j'avais facilement mal à la tête.

Cette atmosphère de fête m'irritait et me fatiguait. Je pris congé. La maîtresse de maison me prévint que la minuterie était détraquée et que l'ascenseur était en panne lui aussi.

—Je peux vous faire un peu de lumière, attendez.

—De la lumière, vous plaisantez, lui dis-je, je suis comme les chats, moi, je vois clair la nuit.

—Vous entendez, dit-elle à ses amis, il est comme les chats, c'est merveilleux, il voit clair la nuit.

Pourquoi avais-je dit cela, une façon de parler, une phrase polie et qui se voulait spirituelle, dégagée.

Je commençais à descendre péniblement les premières marches de l'escalier et les petites barres de cuivre du tapis faisaient un bruit curieux sous mes pas qui glissaient.

J'étais dans une si noire obscurité que j'eus d'abord envie de remonter et d'appeler.

Je fouillais d'abord mes poches, mais vainement, pas d'allumettes.

Je m'assis et réfléchis, à quoi, je ne sais plus, j'attendais peut-être que quelqu'un vînt à mon secours sans, bien entendu, savoir ou deviner que j'avais besoin d'aide.

Me relevant péniblement et ne trouvant pas la rampe, je me heurtais violemment contre un mur et me mis à saigner du nez.

Cherchant dans mes poches un mouchoir, je mis enfin la main sur une boîte d'allumettes avec, fort malencontreusement, une seule allumette dedans.

CONFESSIONS OF A MAN CONDEMNED

Why did they cut my head off?
I can admit it now, everything fades with time as they say.
Really, it was so simple.
I had gone to spend the evening with friends, at their place, but
  there was a big crowd and it was a bore. Back then I tended to
  be rather depressed and I got a lot of headaches.
The party atmosphere was getting on my nerves and I decided to
  leave. The hostess informed me that the electricity in the stair-
  well was out and the lights didn't work. The elevator either.
"I can light your way down if you give me a moment."
"Light my way," I replied. "You've got to be joking. I'm like a cat. I
  see in the dark."
"You hear that?" she said to her guests. "He's like a cat. He sees in
  the dark."
What made me tell her such a thing? Just something to say, I guess.
  A polite little pleasantry, witty and casual.
So I started down the stairs, though not without difficulty, and my
  steps made a funny little swishing sound as they slid along the
  thin copper strips that nailed down the carpeting.
Everything around me was so totally black that at first I was
  tempted to go back up and call out.
I rummaged in my pockets, but no use, no matches.
I sat down and began to think. What about, I really don't remember.
  Maybe I was waiting for someone to show up and come to the
  rescue, though without the slightest suspicion, of course, that I
  needed help.
I staggered to my feet and felt here and there trying to find the ban-
  ister. Instead, I went smashing headlong into a wall. My nose
  began to bleed.
I reached in my pocket for a handkerchief and finally came across
  a box of matches. Unfortunately, there was just one left.

Je l'allumai avec d'infinies précautions et, cherchant une nouvelle fois la rampe, j'aperçus d'abord dans un miroir, sur le palier de l'étage où je m'étais arrêté, mon visage couvert de sang.

Et ce fut à nouveau l'obscurité.

Je me trouvais de plus en plus désemparé.

Soudain, étendant au hasard, à tâtons, la main, je touchai un serpent qui se mit à glisser.

Charmante soirée.

Ce serpent, c'était tout simplement la rampe que par bonheur j'avais retrouvée et qui rampait doucement sous ma main qui venait d'essuyer mon visage si stupidement ensanglanté.

Je me mis alors à rire: j'étais sauvé.

Et comme je descendais allègrement mais prudemment, je fus tout à coup renversé par quelqu'un ou quelque chose qui, à toute vitesse, lui ou elle aussi, descendait en même temps qu'une petite flamme, sans aucun doute celle d'un briquet.

Me relevant encore une fois, je marchai à nouveau dans le noir, mes deux mains devant moi.

Ces deux mains rencontrèrent le mur et le mur céda…

Ce n'était pas le mur mais une porte entrouverte.

Soudain de la musique et de la lumière venant des étages supérieurs!

Sans aucun doute des invités qui, à leur tour, descendaient et que la maîtresse de maison accompagnait, un flambeau à la main.

Vraiment, je ne savais où me mettre et ce n'était pas une façon de parler; aussi, profitant de cette porte pour me dissimuler, je pénétrai plus avant, quand tout à coup, dans la lumière qui grandissait, je découvris un corps étendu à mes pieds.

C'était le corps d'Antoinette.

Elle était là, couchée, les yeux ouverts, la gorge aussi.

Antoinette avec qui j'avais vécu si longtemps et qui, le mois dernier, m'avait abandonné.

I lit it with the utmost care and, as I tried again to find the banister,
   I suddenly caught sight of myself in a mirror on the landing
   where I had stopped. My face was smeared with blood.
Then everything went black again.
I was growing more and more desperate.
Suddenly, as I reached out, feeling here and there, my hand touched
   a snake that began to slide and slither.
Delightful evening.
The snake was actually the banister. I had somehow found it, and
   it was slithering gently beneath my hand that had just wiped
   my face covered with all that stupid blood.
I started to laugh. I was saved.
Then, just as I was briskly but cautiously feeling my way down the
   stairs, all of a sudden I was knocked over by someone or some-
   thing barreling down, and holding in his her or its hand a little
   flame, no doubt from a lighter.
I got up again and padded about in the dark, with both hands out-
   stretched.
Those hands hit the wall and the wall gave way...
Except that it wasn't a wall at all, but a door standing ajar.
Suddenly, music and light from the upper floors!
No doubt some of the guests, about to come down too, with the
   hostess leading the way, candle in hand.
Really, I didn't know where to turn. And that's not just a manner
   of speaking, either. So, taking advantage of that door to hide
   behind, I went on in, when, all of a sudden, thanks to the light,
   which was getting stronger and stronger, I looked down and
   saw a corpse lying at my feet.
It was Antoinette's.
There she was, stretched out, her eyes gaping wide, and her throat
   no less so.
Antoinette, the woman I had lived with for so long and who, just
   last month, had thrown me over.

Antoinette que j'avais suppliée, que j'avais même menacée.

Je ne pus retenir un cri.

De terreur, ce cri et de stupeur aussi.

La maîtresse de maison, les invités se précipitent, des portes s'ou-
vrent, d'autres lumières bientôt se mêlent à la leur, portées par
d'autres locataires déshabillés, terrorisés et blêmes.

Beaucoup de temps déjà s'était écoulé depuis que j'avais pris congé
et j'étais là, muet et couvert de sang, hagard comme dans les
pires histoires.

Près du corps de mon amie perdue et—en quel état—retrouvée, sur
le parquet, une lame luisait comme un morceau de lune dans
un ciel étoilé.

Dans chaque main tremblante une lumière bougeait.

Présence inexplicable ou bien trop expliquée.

Vous voyez d'ici le procès: le pourvoi rejeté, le petit verre, le crucifix
à embrasser et encore comme une lune, le couperet d'acier.

Que voulez-vous, mettez-vous à ma place. Que pouvais-je dire, que
pouvais-je raconter? J'avais passé un trop mauvais quart d'heure
dans les mornes ténèbres de ce noir escalier et j'avais eu la folle
imprudence d'affirmer: je vois clair la nuit, moi, je suis comme
les chats.

Qui m'aurait cru alors et sans me rire au nez?

Oui, j'en suis sûr, on m'aurait ri au nez pendant de longues, de trop
longues années à mon gré.

J'ai préféré me taire plutôt que d'être ridiculisé.

Antoinette, whom I had pleaded with, and begged, even threatened.
In spite of myself I let out a loud shriek.
A scream of terror and of mind-dulling awe.
All at once the hostess comes running, and the guests. Next moment, doors fly open, other lights join theirs, held by other tenants, half-dressed, pale with horror.
So much time had gone by since I had left the party. And there I was, speechless and covered with blood, wild-eyed, as in the cheapest of novels.
On the floor, next to the body of my mistress, lost and found—and found now in what condition!—a blade was shining like a slice of moon in a starlit sky.
Light flickered from everyone's trembling fingers.
Inexplicable, my presence, or only too well explained.
You can imagine the trial: the appeal rejected, the little glass of water, the crucifix to kiss and swear on, and again, like a moon, the guillotine's blade of steel.
So? What would you have done in my shoes? What could I say, what could I tell them? I had spent such miserable moments in that staircase's dismal shades, and I had been foolhardy enough to boast: I see in the dark. I'm like a cat.
Who would have believed me without laughing in my face?
Yes, no doubt about it, they would have laughed in my face, and I wouldn't have lived it down for years.
I preferred to hold my tongue rather than be made a fool of.

DE VOS JOURS

I

Concomitamment la muture concraite et la peinsique abstrète
vous donnent les belles couleurs de l'amateur et le bon ton du mélo-
mane distingué.

II

Ils font d'abord la sourde oreille
et puis l'œil aveugle
et puis les bras manchots
Un peu plus tard
comme la musique par d'autres est appréciée estampillée consacrée
        et reconnue d'utilité musique
alors ils applaudissent la musique
frénétiquement rageusement
comme s'ils fessaient un enfant.

IN YOUR TIME

I

Concomitantly musète concrique and abstract painting[1]
give you the amateur's beautiful colors and the distinguished *bel
canto* lover's toniness.

II

First they turn a deaf ear
and then a blind eye
and then missing arms
A little later
since music by others is appreciated if hallmarked consecrated and
    recognized as musically useful
they applaud the music
frantically frenetically
as if they were giving a child a spanking.

---

[1] I preserve the allusion—deformed, of course—to the original *"musique concrète"* without giving an English equivalent since it is usually, if not always, in French that the phenomenon brought about by the electronic advances of the 1940s and 50s is discussed.

LE SALON

(Ballet)

C'est l'été.

Un terrassier ivre de joie de vivre, tout simplement, danse sur un trottoir.

Il fait beau, c'est le soir et le goût du bonheur et le désir d'amour lui font oublier l'heure.

Est-ce sa jeunesse qui le fait danser ou bien lui qui fait danser sa jeunesse pour lui faire oublier la fatigue du chantier, on ne sait.

Soudain, il s'arrête net devant la porte d'un bel hôtel particulier.

Sous le porche, une lanterne au dernier goût du jour, piquante vulgarité très Saint-Germain-des-Prés, d'une lumière un peu rouge éclaire l'entrée.

Le terrassier cligne de l'œil du connaisseur devant cette engageante et clignotante lueur.

Un souvenir tout simple caresse sa mémoire : fées nues, déesses intéressées mais si faciles à aimer, à caresser.

Il franchit le porche, très à l'aise, comme chez lui.

Des loufiats aux mollets gainés de blanc le laissent passer un peu surpris, mais ils en ont vu d'autres et peut-être qu'on donne ici ce soir aussi un bal travesti.

Des invités en habit et robe du soir ou en impeccable négligé entourent le maître et la maîtresse de maison.

La maîtresse de maison est belle et le maître de maison assez singulièrement beau garçon.

Tout le monde boit du champagne.

Les dames sont très décolletées, c'est-à-dire aux trois quarts nues, enfin le plus possible.

THE SALON

(Ballet)

It's summer.

A road-digger full of spunk and drunk on life is dancing on a sidewalk.

It's a lovely evening and his taste for joy and his yearning for love make him forget the hour.

Is it his youth that makes him dance or—who can say—does he set his youth dancing to make it forget the strains and pains of his labors?

All at once he stops short before the door of a fine private dwelling.

Hanging from the front, a lantern of vulgar modishness, very piquantly Saint-Germain-des-Prés, casts a reddish light on the entrance.

The digger winks a knowing wink before that brightly blinking invitation.

His memory is caressed by a simple recollection: fairy maids unclad, goddesses intent on gain but so easy to love, so easy to caress.

Making himself at home, he strides casually in the door.

White-legging-calved flunkies let him pass, not a little bemused, but they have seen their fill of others, and maybe tonight too they're having a masked ball.

Guests in full dress and evening gowns, or attire impeccably informal, surround the host and hostess.

The hostess is beautiful and the host is a most singularly dashing young fellow.

Everyone sips champagne.

The ladies boast necklines exposed as can be, that is, a good three-quarters bare.

Le terrassier qui est beau, comme elles sont belles, ne passe pas inaperçu.

— C'est vraiment du tonnerre, cet audacieux débraillé! dit une très charmante poupée, déshabillée à ravir par un très grand couturier.

Le terrassier s'assoit et fait son choix.

C'est-à-dire que, buvant un verre, il fait signe au loufiat qui le sert, désignant celle sur qui il a jeté son dévolu: la maîtresse de maison.

Le loufiat s'éloigne sans comprendre et la maîtresse de maison, très occupée, n'a même pas vu le terrassier.

Mais le maître de maison, lui, tout de suite l'a remarqué.

Il s'avance vers lui, élégant, minaudant, primesautier et, profitant de l'atmosphère de fête et du brouhaha général, s'assoit sur ses genoux et le prend par le cou en toute intimité.

Le terrassier se lève et le maître de maison tombe.

— Chatouillez la cariatide sous les bras et le monument s'écroulera, dit le terrassier hilare, histoire de faire rire le monde.

Et les invités en dansant répètent ce mot charmant.

Curieuse, surprise et amusée, la maîtresse de maison s'approche.

Le terrassier l'examine de très près, la palpe, la retourne et déçu hoche la tête.

Mais la maîtresse de maison veut à tout prix danser avec ce surprenant invité clandestin et qui est à vrai dire le clou de la soirée.

Résigné, il danse avec « la patronne » parce que ça se fait et comme elle est un peu ivre, perdant toute retenue, elle danse comme on rêve, elle danse à la dérive, rivée au clou de la soirée comme la riveuse à son rivetier.

The digger, as handsome as the ladies are lovely, does not go unnoticed.

"I must say, he's not shy, that one," says a charming doll-like creature, ravishingly underdressed, no doubt, by some great *grand couturier.*

The digger takes a seat and makes his choice.

That is, while sipping, he nods to the flunky serving the champagne, pointing out the one that he deigns to prefer: the hostess herself.

The flunky, with no idea what the digger intends, goes off about his business; as for the hostess, she's too busy to see him.

But her husband, the host, has seen him from the start.

Elegant and poised, he minces impetuously toward him, and, availing himself of the festive mood and the general hubbub, sits down on his lap and, with the greatest of liberties, takes him around the neck.

The digger stands up and the host falls to the floor.

"Tickle the statues that hold up the building and the building comes a-tumbling!" quips the digger, eager to get a laugh from the others.

And they all keep dancing as they repeat his delightful *mot.*

Curious, surprised, and amused, the hostess herself approaches.

The digger inspects her in close detail, presses her flesh, front and back, and, disenchanted, gives a little rejecting shake of the head.

But the hostess, not to be put off, insists on dancing with this secret surprise guest, now the veritable keystone of the *fête,* on whom all eyes and ears are riveted.

Resigned, he dances with "madame" since it's only right after all, and, because she's a little tipsy, she dances as in a dream, a little topsy-turvy, tipping and tripping, and riveted to her keystone like rivet-gun to its riveter.

Le maître de la maison, horriblement jaloux et non seulement de sa femme, trépigne, appelle « ses gens » puis soudain se calme et, soucieux d'éviter le scandale, les renvoie en baissant la voix puis dansant, léger, devant un miroir met un peu d'ordre dans sa toilette avec un petit sourire légèrement chiffonné.

Le terrassier, tout en dansant, le regarde faire, amusé.

Soudain, il découvre dans le miroir l'image d'une camériste qui doucement, un plateau à la main, traverse le salon.

Elle est noire et très belle, belle de partout, noire de Bahia ou de Harlem.

Le terrassier se précipite, abandonnant sa cavalière, renverse le miroir, le plateau et les verres, et fait danser la belle.

Ils oublient tous deux le salon, ils oublient le décor: alors le décor change.

Et ils dansent où ils veulent, sous un ciel étoilé pour eux seuls, ils dansent l'amour qu'ils veulent auprès d'un lit défait et le rideau retombe, épais, lourd et discret.

The host, dreadfully jealous—and not only of his wife—sputters and fumes, summons "his people," then, suddenly eager to avoid a scandal, lowers his voice and sends them away as, light of foot, he dances over to a mirror, and stops to adjust his *toilette* with a slight little smirk.

The digger, still dancing, watches him, amused.

All at once, in the mirror he notices a serving-wench who, tray in hand, is gliding across the room.

She's a black and very beautiful, a black from Bahía or Harlem, very beautiful from wherever...

The digger leaves his partner, goes dashing over, knocks down the mirror, the tray and the glasses, takes the beauty in his arms and goes dancing her about.

Both forget the salon, both forget the décor: now the décor changes.

And they're dancing where they will, beneath a sky studded with stars twinkling just for them, dancing the love they desire beside an unmade bed, and down comes the curtain, thick, heavy, and discreet.

IN MEMORIAM

Il est interdit de faire de la musique plus de vingt-quatre heures
    par jour
ça finira par me faire du tort
Hier au soir un Hindou amnésique
a mis tous mes souvenirs dans une grosse boule en or
et la boule a roulé au fond d'un corridor
et puis dans l'escalier elle a dégringolé
renversant un monsieur
devant la loge de la concierge
un monsieur qui voulait dire son nom en rentrant
Et la boule lui a jeté tous mes souvenirs à la tête
et il a dit mon nom à la place du sien
et maintenant
me voilà bien tranquille pour un bon petit bout de temps
Il a tout pris pour lui
je ne me souviens de rien
et il est parti sangloter sur la tombe de mon grand-père paternel
le judicieux éleveur de sauterelles
l'homme qui ne valait pas grand-chose mais qui n'avait peur de rien
et qui portait des bretelles mauves
Sa femme l'appelait grand vaurien
ou grand saurien peut-être
oui c'est cela je crois bien grand saurien
ou autre chose
est-ce que je sais
est-ce que je me souviens

IN MEMORIAM

It's forbidden to play music more than twenty-four hours a day
it's bound to do me harm in the end
Last night a Hindu amnesiac
packed all my memories into a big golden ball
and the ball rolled down to the end of a hall
and then went tumbling stumbling down the stairs
and bowled over a certain gent
in front of the concierge's stall
a monsieur who meant to give his name at the door
And the ball loosed all my memories at his head
and he didn't say his own name but said mine instead
and now
here I am with nothing to bother me for a nice long while
He took them for himself and made them all his
I don't recall a thing
and he went off to sob on my grandfather's grave
on my father's side that is
the one who bred grasshoppers and did a careful job
who wasn't worth much but who didn't fear a thing
and wore mauve-colored suspenders
His wife used to say he was a lazy slob
and called him a crock of bile
or maybe a crocodile
yes that's it I think a big crocodile
unless it was something else
can I know
can I recall

Tout ça futilités fonds de tiroirs miettes et gravats de ma
    mémoire
Je ne connais plus le fin mot de l'histoire

Et la mémoire
comment est-elle faite la mémoire
de quoi a-t-elle l'air
de quoi aura-t-elle l'air plus tard
la mémoire
Peut-être qu'elle était verte pour les souvenirs de vacances
peut-être que c'est devenu maintenant un grand panier d'osier
    sanglant
avec un petit monde assassiné dedans
et une étiquette avec le mot Haut
avec le mot Bas
et puis le mot Fragile en grosses lettres rouges
ou bleues
ou mauves
pourquoi pas mauves
enfin grises et roses
puisque j'ai le choix maintenant.

All that meaningless stock of junk just scraps left behind in my
     memory-drawer
The point of the story isn't clear anymore

And memory
what is it and what makes it so
what does it seem to be
and what will it seem like presently
this memory thing
Maybe it was green with remembered past vacations
maybe now it's become a bloodied wicker trunk
with a whole little world lying hunkered dead inside
all my assassinations
with a label This Side Up
and one This Side Down
and Fragile in big red letters I think
or blue
or mauve
of course why not mauve
or even gray and pink
since the choice is all mine and no one else's today.

AU FEU ET À L'EAU!

Ils ont crié À l'eau
comme Au feu ou Au fou

L'eau gagnant du terrain
sous son oreiller d'herbes
le cachait dans son lit
tout comme un chien un os
le planque dans son trou
Ils ont crié À l'eau
comme Au voleur on crie

C'est alors qu'arrivèrent
les Grands Bouilleurs de Crue

Descendant de voiture ils incendièrent la ville
et l'eau à toute vapeur disparut dans le ciel
Et la voiture s'en fut avec comme à une bouée
un noyé accroché à sa roue de secours
et dans sa malle arrière un coffre plein d'argent
tout l'argent de la ville
sans aucun survivant.

FIRE AND FLOOD! [1]

They cried out Flood
like Lunatic loose or Fire

The water rose higher
and was hiding the ground
under a pillow of grasses on its bed
like a dog with a bone
who stashes it in his hole
They cried out Flood
and Stop thief was the sound

It was then there came round
the Big Outlaw Flood-Brewers[2]

Stepping from the car they set fire to the city
and the water in a flash steamed off through the air
And the car took off too dragging somebody drowned
still hanging on the spare wheel like on a life preserver
and in the trunk a chest filled with cash
all the city's wealth
and not a survivor anywhere to be found.

---

[1] Ideally, I would put an exclamation point after both nouns, not only the second, as well as in lines 8 and 9 of the text, but I won't second-guess Prévert.

[2] The usual spelling of the French is *"cru,"* a *"bouilleur de cru"* being a clandestine distiller. Barring the unlikelihood of a misprint, Prévert's spelling with an added *-e* could be a play on *"crue"* (flood), as my translation attempts to suggest, somewhat obtusely.

TANT DE FORÊTS...

Tant de forêts arrachées à la terre
et massacrées
achevées
rotativées

Tant de forêts sacrifiées pour la pâte à papier
des milliards de journaux attirant annuellement l'attention des
    lecteurs sur les dangers du déboisement des bois et des forêts.

SO MANY FORESTS...

So many forests wrenched up from the earth
ripped up
hacked up
buzz-sawed up to bits

So many forests yielded up for the pulp
of the billions of newspapers that year after year call their readers'
    attention to the dangers of deforestation of the woods and the
    forests.

---

[1] With the seemingly invented participle *"rotativés"* Prévert is probably referring
to the *"scie rotative"* (high-powered circular saw) used in logging. Given the context,
it is just possible too, though unlikely, that he has in mind the rotary presses (*"ro-
tatives"*) on which newspapers are printed.

L'ENFANT DE MON VIVANT

Dans la plus fastueuse des misères
mon père ma mère
apprirent à vivre à cet enfant
à vivre comme on rêve et jusqu'à ce que mort s'ensuive
naturellement
Sa voix de rares pleurs et de rires fréquents
sa voix me parle encore
sa voix mourante et gaie
intacte et saccagée
Je ne puis le garder je ne puis le chasser
ce gentil revenant
Comment donner le coup de grâce
à ce camarade charmant
qui me regarde dans la glace
et de loin me fait des grimaces
pour me faire marrer
drôlement
et qui m'apprit à faire l'amour
maladroitement
éperdument

L'enfant de mon vivant
sa voix de pluie et de beau temps
chante toujours son chant lunaire ensoleillé
son chant vulgaire envié et méprisé
son chant terre à terre
étoilé

Non
je ne serai jamais leur homme
puisque leur homme est un roseau pensant

CHILD OF THE LIVING LIFE I LED

In the most impoverished of luxuries
my father and my mother
taught that child how to live
to live as one dreams as long as death please
like every other
naturally
His voice fearful at times and happy more often
his voice still speaks to me
his voice gay and intact
or racked and dying
Nice little ghost that I
can neither keep nor chase away
How do you strike the *coup de grâce* to end
the days of such a charming friend
eyeing me in the glass with sly
grimacing faces trying
to tickle me
comically
and who taught me to make love
cumbersomely
desperately

Child of the living life I led
his weather-smalltalk voice still sings
its sunlit moonstruck renderings
its earthy song scorned and yet coveted
its down-to-earth song
starshine-spread

No
never will I be their man
because their man is a thinking reed[1]

non jamais je ne deviendrai cette plante carnivore qui tue son dieu
et le dévore et vous invite à déjeuner et puis si vous refusez vous
accuse de manger du curé
Et j'écoute en souriant l'enfant de mon vivant
l'enfant heureux aimé
et je le vois danser
danser avec ma fille
avant de s'en aller
là où il doit aller.

no I shall never become that plant carnivorous that kills its god
    munches him up devours him down then invites you to lunch
    and if you refuse accuses you of hating the Church with a lusty
    appetite[2]
And I listen and smile
at the child of the living life I led
beloved and happy-spirited
and watch him dancing to and fro
with my daughter for a while
dancing before he must go
where he's got to be going.

---

[1] This is an obvious allusion to Pascal's celebrated dictum that Man, the frailest of reeds, is at least *"un roseau pensant"* (a thinking reed) whose power of thought compensates for his weakness by understanding it.

[2] Prévert plays with the phrase *"manger"* (or, more usually, *"bouffer"*) *"du curé,"* roughly translatable as "to feast on priest" and signifying a distaste for religion.

FATRAS
(1966)

L'ARGUMENT MASSU

Ce n'est pas de gaieté de cœur que nous nous sommes mis l'esprit à la torture pour légitimer la torture.

Nous avons payé de notre personne le droit d'affirmer qu'il serait oiseux et vain de remettre tout en question et de tenter d'agiter encore les marionnettes de la douleur dans les vieux décors de l'horreur.

La question n'est pas là, n'a jamais été là.

La question, c'est la torture. Pourquoi la remettre en question?

On ne torture pas la torture, on ne questionne pas la question.

THE SLEDGEHAMMER ARGUMENT
OF GENERAL MASSU[1]

It's never light-heartedly that we've tortured our minds to argue the case for torture.

With body and soul we've earned the right to affirm that it would be futile and vain to question everything yet again and to try once more to dangle the puppets of pain against the age-old décors of horror.

That's not, and never has been, the question.

The question is torture. Why question it yet again?

Torture ought not be tortured, the question ought not be questioned.

---

[1] The several levels of Prévert's pun are impossible to capture in one or two words. He combines the phrase *"argument massue"* (sledgehammer—i.e., decisive—argument) with the name of General Jacques Massu, one of the principals in the Algerian War (1954–62), around whom the question of the legitimacy of torture in war raged at the time. It is interesting to note that ten years ago the nonagenarian Massu admitted to the frequent use of torture by French troops in Algeria but denied any responsibility for it. (See *Le Monde,* 22 June 2000.)

ET LES CABIRES ONT DANSÉ

La victoire de Samothrace
Vénus d'un coup de pied l'a décapitée
Et les restes de sa défaite
gisent au fond de la mer Égée.

AND THE CABIRI DID A DANCE[1]

Beheaded was the Victory
Of Samothrace, by Venus kicked
Other spoils of defeat lie derelict
Deep down in the Aegean Sea.

---

[1]The two—and, later, several—Cabiri, inherited from Phrygia, were originally mystic fertility divinities especially important on the island of Samothrace several centuries BCE, and eventually incorporated into the Greek pantheon.

Quand la vie est un collier
chaque jour est une perle
Quand la vie est une cage
chaque jour est une larme
Quand la vie est une forêt
chaque jour est un arbre
Quand la vie est un arbre
chaque jour est une branche
Quand la vie est une branche
chaque jour est une feuille

Quand la vie c'est la mer
chaque jour est une vague
chaque vague une plainte
une chanson un frisson
Quand la vie est un jeu
chaque jour est une carte
le carreau ou le trèfle
le pique le malheur
Et quand c'est le bonheur
les cartes de l'amour
c'est le cul et le cœur.

When life is a necklace
each day is a bead
When life is a cage
each day is a tear
When life is a forest
each day is a tree
When life is a tree
each day is a branch
When life is a branch
each day is a leaf

When life is the sea
each day is a wave
each wave a lament
a song a shudder
When life is a deck
each day's a playing-card
the diamond the club
the spade of distress
And when it's happiness
the cards of love
are the heart and the ass.

RÊVE

Quelque part où il y a la mer
—dans le rêve je sais où c'est—
une fille nue
sans être remarquée
traverse une foule tout habillée
Elle me surprend sans me troubler
C'est d'abord cela mon rêve
mais soudain je vois ma mère
dans une grande voiture d'un autrefois encore récent
une voiture pour Noces et Banquets
avec les chevaux le cocher
La mariée c'est ma mère
Est-elle en blanc
je n'en sais plus rien maintenant
Près d'elle il y a mon père
ou peut-être que je l'ajoute maintenant
Et ma mère m'aperçoit
et sourit de son sourire toujours enfant
mais elle a pour moi en même temps
un regard de tendre et douloureux reproche
Je n'ai pas d'excuse
j'aurais dû aller à son mariage
Bien sûr je n'étais pas invité
Je suis de la famille et on m'attendait
maintenant il est trop tard

DREAM

Someplace by a somewhere sea—
in the dream I knew just where—
a naked maid
walks through a crowd all fully dressed
She comes upon me quietly
And that at first is all the dream
but suddenly what do I see
my mother in a great van of the recent past
a large Weddings and Banquets van
but also a kind of coach-and-four
And my mother is the bride
She's dressed all in white
and that's all I can remember now
And my father is sitting close beside
or maybe that's something I'm adding now
And my mother sees me catches sight
and smiles her simple childlike smile
but still she gives me all the while
a look of tender pained reproachfulness
I have no excuse
I guess I should have gone to the wedding
But I wasn't invited I'm sure you know
I'm part of the family and I was expected
now it's too late

la fête est passée
et ce n'était pas pour moi
la moindre mais la plus pressante des choses à faire
Je ne l'ai pas faite.

(11 décembre 1960, 4 heures le matin.)

the party is over before I knew it
and going to it would have been for me
not the least but the most important of things to do
And I didn't do it.[1]

(11 December 1960, 4 a.m.)

---

[1] My wordplay in the last four lines tries to suggest, with different elements, Prévert's evident punning on *"fête"* and *"faite."*

Un homme et une femme
jamais ne se sont vus
Ils vivent très loin l'un de l'autre
et dans des villes différentes
Un jour
ils lisent la même page d'un même livre
en même temps
à la seconde seconde
de la première minute
de leur dernière heure
exactement.

A man and a woman
have never met
They live in different cities
far away from each other
One day
they're reading the same page of the same book
at the same time
the second second
of the first minute
of their final hour
exactly.

Toute réflexion faite
par ces temps de malheur
le miroir s'est brisé.

After due reflection
on these ill-gotten times
the mirror up and broke.

Les sorciers
lorsqu'ils font de terrifiantes conneries
on accuse toujours l'apprenti.

When sorcerer
pulls horrid ass-hole blunders it's
monsieur's assistant who must take the hits.

Je suis heureuse
Il m'a dit hier
qu'il m'aimait
Je suis heureuse et fière
et libre comme le jour
Il n'a pas ajouté
que c'était pour toujours.

Says she I'm glad to say[1]
that yesterday
he said he was in love with me
I'm proud and glad
and free as air however
He never thought to add
that it was for forever.

---

[1] Here, as in other examples (see notes, pages 165 and 303), a phrase has to be added—unobtrusively, I hope—to make the poem as gender-specific in English as it is in French.

Et Dieu
surprenant Adam et Ève
leur dit
Continuez je vous en prie
ne vous dérangez pas pour moi
Faites comme si je n'existais pas.

And God
walking in on Eve and Adam
says: Sir, Madam
no need to stop for me I insist
please don't let me interrupt
Just make believe I don't exist.

LA PRINCIPAUTÉ DES POÈTES

Quelles images envoient-ils
dans la glace
qui leur renvoie de telles
grimaces?

THE PRINCIPALITY OF POETS

Thrown at the mirror what must be
their images
if it sends back to them
such grimaces?

Le chat vit beaucoup moins longtemps que l'homme
Qu'importe s'il vit davantage
Mais les chevaux meurent à vingt ans.

The cat lives a much shorter time than man
What does it matter if he lives longer
But horses die when they're twenty.[1]

---

[1] Not calculated to please cat lovers, these lines, typical of Prévert's frequently cryptic brevity, seem to suggest that, even if the cat lived as long as the horse, its usefulness to man would be debatable.

EST-CE PASSE-TEMPS?

Est-ce passe-temps d'écrire
est-ce passe-temps de rêver
Cette page
était toute blanche
il y a quelques secondes
Une minute
ne s'est pas encore écoulée
Maintenant voilà qui est fait.

IS IT A PASTIME?

Is it a pastime to write
is it a pastime to dream
This page
was all white
a few seconds ago
Not a minute
has gone by
And now so much for that.

ARAGNE LE PEINTRE

Il peint une toile sur une toile
et attend qu'on lui parle de cette toile.
Dès qu'on lui en parle
dès que quelqu'un
n'importe qui
lui donne son avis
il prend la mouche
et l'écrase sur la toile peinte en noir sur la toile
Il signe cette toile
et le soir il l'appelle espoir
le matin il l'appelle chagrin
et le tantôt il l'expose
et s'il la vend l'appelle cadeau.

ARACHNE THE PAINTER[1]

The painter paints a web in a painting[2]
and waits for people to comment on them both
As soon as they do
as soon as someone
no matter who
gives him an opinion
he takes a fly
flies into a snit[3]
and crushes it on the web painted black in the painting
He signs the painting
and at night he calls it hope[4]
in the morning he calls it trouble
and in the afternoon he shows it
and if he sells it he calls it gift.

---

[1] Classicists and even others may recall that Minerva, challenged in a contest of needlework, bested the skillful seamstress Arachne, who, despondent, hanged herself and was turned by the goddess into a spider.

[2] Both *toiles*, that is. The double meaning of the word (web and canvas) requires a little finagling in translation.

[3] Prévert puns here on the expression *"prendre la mouche"* (to take offense), to be understood both literally and figuratively.

[4] According to French superstition, spiders bring bad luck in the morning (*"Araignée le matin, chagrin"*) and good luck in the evening (*"Araignée le soir, espoir"*).

D'APRÈS NATURE

Cette fleur n'est pas sortie du sable
comme ce verre
Ce verre n'est pas sorti de terre
comme cette fleur
La main qui modela ce vase
et l'autre main ailleurs qui cueillit cette fleur
ne sortaient ni de côte d'Adam ni de cuisse de Jupiter
ni d'aucune autre boîte de prestidigitateur
Et ces mains en allées
d'où venaient-elles alors
où allaient-elles encore
Et cette céramique
et cette pièce de bois
et ce morceau de cuir
et cette petite punaise sur cette croix d'honneur

Le vent déplace les dunes
le temps efface les monuments
Et chacun s'en va avec sa chacune
et disparaît et reparaît
et se retrouve et s'ignore
alternativement
en toute simplicité
comme sang dans les veines
poisson dans la mer
arête dans le gosier.

NATURE'S LAW

This flower was not born of the sand
as was this glass
this glass was not born of the soil
as was this flower
The hand that gave this vase its shape
and the other hand that picked this flower
were neither born from Adam's rib or Jupiter's thigh
or the bag of tricks of some stage sorcerer
And those hands now gone off
where did they come from
where did they fly
And this ceramic chip
this bit of wood
this leather strip
this little tack to fix the *croix d'honneur*

The winds displace the dune-born sands
time will efface the monuments
Couples go fleeting hands in hands
disappear reappear in inverse sense
may know each other or may not
casually
simple as nature's law
like blood in the veins
fish in the sea
fishbone sticking in the craw.

L'ÉTOILE DE MER

L'étoile
quand on la rejette à la mer
disparaît en dansant
c'est un petit rat d'Opéra
Toujours une tête
deux jambes
deux bras.

THE STARFISH

The starfish
when you throw it back
like little Opéra twinkle-toes
dances a bit
disappears and so it goes
Always one head
two arms two legs
That's it.

LA FÊTE SECRÈTE

Au carrefour impossible de l'immobilité
une foule d'objets inertes
ne cesse de remuer de frémir de danser
Et les facteurs du vent
comme ceux de la marée
éparpillent le courrier
Chaque chose sans doute est destinée à quelqu'un ou
    à quelque chose peut-être
La plume de l'oiseau
comme l'écaille de l'huître
la croix de la légion d'honneur
comme l'étoile de mer
ou la patte du crabe et l'ancre du navire
la grenouille de fer vert
et la poupée de son
et le collier de chien
Et dans ce paysage où rien ne semble bouger
sauf la bougie du naufrageur dans la lanterne rouillée
c'est la fête secrète
la fête des objets.

THE SECRET PARTY

Here where the impossible crosses the motionless
a crowd of lifeless things
shakes quivers dances endlessly
And the couriers of the wind
like those of the tide
scatter far and wide the mail
Each object is meant for someone or destined perhaps
    for something
The quill of the bird
and the scaly oyster shell
the cross of the Legion of Honor
and the starfish
or the leg of the crab and the anchor of the ship
the green iron frog
and the little stuffed doll
the collar of a dog
And in this landscape where nothing seems to move
save for the flicker of the wrecker's wick in his rusty lantern
it's a secret party
the party of lifeless things.

CHOSES ET AUTRES

(1972)

SAIT-ON JAMAIS?

Eux disent savoir toujours
Ils disent la terre la lune le cosmos l'infini le bien le mal
    et les origines de la vie
Ils disent tout comme si de rien n'était
mais quand l'appréhension de l'incompréhension les prend
ils prennent peur
et cette peur renverse la vapeur de leurs idées
Alors ils s'arrêtent à la première gare
à la première station standard
Et c'est toujours le même horaire la même horreur celle du vide
Alors ils font leur plein d'essence divine
démarrent à nouveau
et s'en vont de plus en plus vite
pour arriver de moins en moins loin.

WHO KNOWS?

They're the ones who always say they know
They say earth moon cosmos infinity good evil and the origins
  of life
They say everything as if it were as simple as could be
but when the frightful insight of their uninsightfulness
  strikes them
they're struck with fear
and that fear turns them round and steams them back
So they stop at the first station
the first service pumps
And it's always the same
the timely horror of the vacuum abhorred
the emptiness
So they gas up their tank with the fuel divine
start the motor again
take off and go driving faster and faster
to get closer and closer to where they first began.

MALGRÉ MOI...

Embauché malgré moi dans l'usine à idées
j'ai refusé de pointer
Mobilisé de même dans l'armée des idées
j'ai déserté
Je n'ai jamais compris grand-chose
Il n'y a jamais grand-chose
ni petite chose
Il y a autre chose.

Autre chose
c'est ce que j'aime qui me plaît
et que je fais.

AGAINST MY WILL...

Put to work against my will in the idea plant
I refused to show up
And likewise drafted into the idea army
I deserted
I've never understood many things
There never are many things
or little anythings
Only other things.

Other things
that's what I fancy *entre nous*
and what I do.

NATALITÉ

La tête en bas
Nathalie hurle
un médecin la tient par un pied

Nathalie hurle à la vie
elle est contre
et compte à rebours
ses secondes premières
ses premières secondes

Nathalie hurle
Ça commence!

Si ce n'était que cela

Nouvelle-née
horrifiée
ce petit être hurle peut-être
Ça recommence!

NATALITY

Head hanging down
Natalie's bawling
a doctor holds her dangling by a foot

Natalie's bawling at life
she's against it
in a countdown counting
down to the first
the first of her seconds

Natalie's bawling
The beginning!

If only that were all

Neo-natally
panicky
maybe the little baby's bawling
Another beginning!

À L'IMPROVISTE

Moi aussi je suis le fils de l'homme
quand je suis né ma mère n'était pas là
Où était-elle?
Au marché peut-être ou chez les voisins
pour leur emprunter du pain et du vin
En son absence mon père a fait l'impossible
pour faire le nécessaire
et il a paraît-il beaucoup souffert
Mais qu'est-ce que ça peut faire
Tant de gens avant lui et depuis ont souffert sous
    Ponce Pilate Napoléon Bonaparte César Borgia
    Salazar Franco Staline Luther ou Adolf Hitler.

UNPREPARED

I'm the son of man too
when I was born my mother was away
Where was she?
At the market maybe or at the neighbors'
asking for the loan of some bread and wine
While she was gone my father bent over backwards
to do what had to be done
and you can bet he suffered plenty
But what difference does it make
So many people before him and since suffered under
    Pontius Pilate Napoleon Bonaparte Caesar Borgia
    Salazar Franco Stalin Luther or Adolf Hitler.[1]

---

[1] Of all the "celebrities" cited, only Portugal's Antonio Salazar (1889–1970) might be unfamiliar to today's readers.

ET TA SŒUR?

C'est la beauté,
dit la détresse,

La volupté,
dit la douleur,

La cruauté,
dit la tendresse,

L'indifférence,
dit le désespoir.

La mort,
dit le malheur.

Ma sœur,
c'est l'amour,
dit l'heur
le bon heur

TELL ME ANOTHER, SISTER!

It's beauty,
says distress,

Lustfulness,
says pain,

Torment,
says tenderness,

Indifference,
says despair.

Death,
says bad luck.

My eye, my sister,[1]
it's love,
says luck,
happy-go-lucky
luck.

---

[1] If the reader wonders what a supposed sister is doing here and in the title, it should be noted that *"Et ta sœur?"* (And your sister?) is roughly the sarcastic French equivalent of "Tell it to the Marines!"

HOMMAGE AU LIT

Jamais il n'est dit
dans leurs litanies
et jamais n'est lu
dans leurs homélies
Toujours la Sainte-Table
toujours le Saint-Siège
jamais le saint-lit
dans l'immobilier
de leur liturgie

O ma jolie
c'est la magie du lit
et grâce à elle
l'amour l'échappe belle.

HOMAGE TO THE BED

Never is the bed
embedded in their litanies[1]
never is it read
in their homilies
Always the Holy-Table
always the Holy-See
the seat of sanctity[2]
never the holy-bed
embedded in their properties'
sacrosanct liturgies

O *ma belle*
it's the bed's sorcery
that truth to tell
lets love go cot-free.[3]

---

[1] I try at least to suggest the untranslatable pun presented by *"lit"* (bed) in *litanies*. Likewise in *liturgies*, below.

[2] I add a line here to accommodate the religious and concrete meanings of *"siège"* (seat), conflated in the French but unclear in the English "Holy See."

[3] For my outrageous "go cot-free," I invoke the principle of the compensatory pun—free-ranging wordplay where precise correspondence is impossible.

LES BAS-RELIEFS DU FESTIN

Les années ont passé, la table est desservie, presque tous les convives sont morts et quelques-uns à la guerre, mais sur la nappe des souvenirs, pour quelques-uns encore vivants, les arlequins de la mémoire dansent le reste du temps.

THE LEFTOVERS' BAS-RELIEF[1]

The years have gone by, the table is cleared, almost all the guests are dead and a few are at war, but on memory's table-linen, for a few still alive, the harlequins of recollection dance away what's left of time.

---

[1] Despite the seriousness of the subject Prévert can't resist a pun on *"reliefs"* (left-overs) appropriate to the context.

CATAIRE

Ils ont insulté les vaches
ils ont insulté les gorilles
les poulets
Ils ont insulté les veaux
ils ont insulté les oies les serins les cochons
    les maquereaux les chameaux
ils ont insulté les chiens
Les chats
ils n'ont pas osé.

CATTALE[1]

They've used them all for insults
cows for fat slobs
gorillas for goons
chickens for cops
They've wept like calves
they've been silly as geese featherbrained as canaries
    filthy as pigs
they've been mackerels—pimps
camels—old sluts
they've been dogs—ugly mutts
But cats
they wouldn't dare.

---

[1] In addition to taking a few necessary interpretive liberties by rearranging French
animal metaphors with English equivalents, I second-guess Prévert here. *"Cataire"*
is actually an uncommon word for catnip.

CHARADE

LE ROI

Fais-moi rire, bouffon.

LE BOUFFON

Sire, votre premier ministre est un imbécile, Votre second ministre un idiot, votre troisième ministere un crétin, votre quartrième minister ...

LE ROI
(saisi de grand hilarité)

Arrête, bouffon, et dis-moi la solution.

LE BOUFFON

La solution, Sire: vous êtes le roi des cons.

CHARADE

THE KING

Make me laugh, jester.

THE JESTER

Sire, your prime minister is an imbecile, your deputy prime minister an idiot, your deputy deputy prime minister a cretin, your deputy deputy deputy...

THE KING
(with a great gale of laughter)

Enough, jester. Get to the point.

THE JESTER

The point, Sire: the point is that Your Majesty is the king of assholes.

LES ENFANTS EXIGEANTS

Pères
regardez-vous à gauche
regardez-vous à droite
Pères
regardez-vous dans la glace
et regardez-nous en face.

CHILDHOOD DEMANDS

Fathers
look at yourselves on the left
look at yourselves on the right
Fathers
look at yourselves in the glass
and look at us flush in the light.

HOMÉLIE-MÉLO

Péremptoire, dans sa chaire, un vertical parle à des assis sur leurs chaises.

Et c'est toujours le même crime passionnel, le même haut fait divers avec les clous, la croix, les épines, l'éponge, le vinaigre, les saintes femmes, le bon et le mauvais gangster, le traître, le tonnerre et les éclairs.

Les assis l'écoutent avec une patience d'ange mais, sur les dalles, des grincements de pieds de chaise témoignent qu'ils font preuve en même temps d'une impatience du diable.

Le suspense du récit du supplice leur semble plus long que le supplice lui-même.

Ils connaissent l'histoire et savent que « ça finit bien puisque le héros ressuscite à la fin ».

HOMILY-MELODRAMA

Peremptorily, *ex cathedra*, an upstanding monsieur is recounting a story to those seated on their chairs.

And it's always the same crime of passion, the same item of "News in (not so) Brief," with the nails, the cross, the thorns, the sponge, the vinegar, the saintly ladies, the good criminal and the bad, the traitor, the thunderclaps and the lightningbolts.

In their seats they listen with angelic patience, but the squeaking of chair legs against the flagstoned floor gives proof at the same time that they're impatient as the devil.

The suspense of the tale of torture seems longer to them than the torture itself.

They're familiar with the story and they know that "it has a happy ending since the hero comes back to life when it's over."

LE BON JEUNE TEMPS

Les rivières étaient claires
la mer était propre
le pain était bon
les saisons saisonnières
les guerres oubliées
et l'amour aimé.

THE GOOD YOUNG DAYS

The streams were clear
the sea was clean
the bread was good
the seasons came as seasons should
and war no more was spoken of
and we loved love.

UNE DENT

Ils ont une dent contre la vie
    et disent que tout est poussière
Ils ont une dent contre la vie
    et plus tard tout un râtelier
Alors ils mordent la poussière
    et la poussière leur rit au nez
La poussière ensoleillée.

A BONE TO PICK[1]

They've got a bone to pick with life
    they say it's nothing only dust
They've got a bone to pick with life
    in time they'll have the whole skeleton
And when at last they bite the dust
    the dust laughs in their face and just
Glistens all golden in the sun.

---

[1] The English equivalent of *"avoir"* (or garder) *"une dent"* (a tooth) *"contre quelqu'un"*
is "to have a bone to pick with someone." Hence my non-literal adaptation, in
which "bone" is to "tooth" as "skeleton" is to "denture" (*"râtelier"*).

SANS FAUTE

(Codicille)

C'est ma faute
c'est ma faute
c'est ma très grande faute d'orthographe
voilà comment j'écris
giraffe.

J'ai eu tort d'avoir écrit cela autrefois
je n'avais pas à me culpabiliser
je n'avais fait aucune phaute d'orthografe
j'avais simplement écrit giraffe en anglais.

FAULTLESS

(Appendix)[1]

The fault is mine
the fault is mine
mine is the frightful spelling gaffe
this is the way I write
giraffe.

I was wrong when I wrote that in the past
there was no fault I didn't have to rue it
I hadn't made a phrightphul spelling gaffe
I'd only spelled *girafe* as the Brits do it.

---

[1] See p. 131.

LES GRANDES FORTUNES

Self père et self fils, il est parti de rien et s'est fait lui-même.
Milliardaire d'ères, il n'a pas de compte à rendre à personne, le temps qu'il a créé c'est de l'argent et l'espace c'est de l'or.
Et les bénéfices c'est de la merde.

THE GREAT FORTUNES

Self-made father, self-made son, he started with zero and built his life single-handed.

Epic epochal billionaire, he owes no one an explanation: the time he created is money, and the space is so much gold.

And the profits, a pile of shit.

FUTURALISME

Dans les corridors suburbains de la Supercité, les agents de l'Intelligence publique demanderont aux passants, s'il en reste, leurs « idées », leur permis d'idéologie surveillée et, dans la plupart des cas, leur « uit » (unique idée tolérée).

Ceux qui ne seront pas en règle seront appréhendés et dirigés vers le bloc opératoire culturel et universel.

L'élucubrator les conduira au greffe de la culpabilité collective et de la responsabilité dirigée.

Là, les grands manipulateurs leur perforeront le ticket socio-cérébral et ils seront remis en liberté maniable, manœuvrable et manutentionnée.

FUTURALISM

In the suburban corridors of the Supercity, the agents of Public Intelligence will interrogate the passers-by, if there are any left, for their "ideas," and will request to be shown their monitored ideology permit and, in most cases, their SPI (sole permissible idea) pass.

Those whose papers are not in order will be taken in tow and directed toward the cultural and universal operational block.

The mind-inspector will escort them to the division of collective guilt and regulated responsibility.

There, the master manipulators will punch their sociocerebral tickets, after which they will be returned to a life of manageable, maneuverable, and well-manipulated freedom.

PRÉNATAL

Bientôt ou un peu plus tard, grâce aux incessants et étonnants progrès de savants génétiques poursuivant sans merci les chromosomes géniques, dès leur prénatalité, les hommes de génie seront sélectionnés et, quelle que soit leur vocation, militaire, mystique ou philosophique, le jour même de leur naissance pourra être, suivant le cas, déclaré Fête Nationale, ce qui ne portera nul préjudice au Deuil National qui, toujours selon l'usage, sera célébré en son temps.

PRENATAL

Soon or a little later, thanks to the unending and astonishing progress of genetic scientists' merciless tracking of the genic chromosomes, men of genius, even before their birth, will be selected out and, whatever their calling—military, mystical, or philosophical—the day of their birth will be accordingly declarable a National Holiday, in no way interfering, however, with the National Day of Mourning, which, in keeping with long tradition, will continue to be observed at its usual time.[1]

---

[1] It is hardly necessary today to call attention to the accuracy of Prévert's 1972 prognosis, ironic though it is.

DÉCÈS

Il est mort, pourquoi irais-je à son enterrement
Puisque, j'en suis certain, il n'ira pas au mien?

DECEASE

He's dead, but why should I go to his funeral
since I'm perfectly sure that he won't go to mine?

LA REVUE

Un enfant (regardant le défilé):
    Où vont-ils?
Un monsieur décoré, trépidant et enthousiasmé:
    Rendre la Bastille!

(14 juillet 1968)

THE REVIEW

A child (watching the parade):
      Where are they going?
A bemedaled monsieur, quivering fervently:
      To give back the Bastille!

(14 July 1968)[1]

---

[1] While the violent student and worker protests of May 1968 had gradually abated, Bastille Day in the Latin Quarter that year saw a resurgence of leftist and anarchist demonstrations. Considerable bloodshed resulted, even among the tourists who had come to Paris for the holiday.

FÊTES À SOUHAITER
... SI L'HISTOIRE SUIT SON COURS

1979: centenaire de Staline.
1983: centenaire de Mussolini.
1989: centenaire de Salazar.
1990: centenaire de De Gaulle.
1992: centenaire de Franco.
2069: tricentenaire de Napoléon Ier.

BIRTHDAYS TO CELEBRATE
... IF HISTORY PROCEEDS AS PLANNED[1]

1979: Stalin's centenary.
1983: Mussolini's centenary.
1989: Salazar's centenary.[2]
1990: De Gaulle's centenary.
1992: Franco's centenary.
2069: Napoleon the First's tricentenary.

---

[1] The reader should keep in mind that all of these anniversary dates—not only the last—were still well in the future in 1972, when the collection *Choses et autres* was published.

[2] See p. 375, note 1.

SOLEIL DE NUIT

(POST.)

VOYAGE DANS LA LUNE

Ah! vous allez là-bas
Oui
Vous savez où c'est?
Non mais je connais
Et vous emmenez tous ces bagages?
Oui
Jamais jamais
Vous entendez
Jamais vous n'arriverez
Là-bas
Avec tout ça

TRIP TO THE MOON

Ah! you're going up there
Yes
And you're sure you know where?
No but I'll know it
And all that baggage?
You're going to take it?
Yes
Never never
You hear
You'll never make it
Up there
With all that gear.

LE MAGASIN

I

Le nez collé contre la vitrine d'un magasin de curiosités, un nain, curieux, regarde une femme debout au milieu du magasin complètement vide.

D'autres curieux s'approchent à leur tour.

Un incurieux passe sans s'arrêter puis gagne un café, le café du Théâtre, afin de boire un café avant d'aller voir au théâtre si le spectacle lui plaît.

II

Au théâtre où le rideau est levé l'incurieux entre et prend place.

Le décor représente l'intérieur d'un magasin de curiosités complètement vide.

Une actrice, immobile au milieu du décor, présente aux spectateurs un objet curieux: un nez de nain collé contre un morceau de vitre cassée ensanglantée.

UN SPECTATEUR (à l'incurieux): Curieux spectacle!

L'INCURIEUX: Vous trouvez?

Il hausse les épaules, se lève et s'en va.

L'ACTRICE: Mesdames et messieurs; la pièce que d'ici une heure ou deux nous aurons eu l'honneur de représenter devant vous s'appelle « la curiosité punie ».

III

Assis sur le trottoir, devant la vitrine brisée du magasin de curiosités sanglote un nain sans nez.

À pas lents sur la chaussée s'avance l'incurieux qui jette un regard de mépris sur le nain sans nez.

THE SHOP

I

With his nose pressed flat against a curio shop window, a dwarf, curious, looks at a woman standing in the middle of the utterly empty store.

Other curious onlookers come by one by one.

An uncurious monsieur passes by without stopping and heads straight for a café, the Café du Théâtre, for a coffee before he goes to the theater to see if he likes the show.

II

The uncurious monsieur goes into the theater, where the curtain has gone up, and takes his seat.

The set represents a curio shop, inside, and utterly empty.

An actress, standing motionless in the middle of the set, holds out a curious object to the audience: a dwarf's nose pressed flat against a piece of glass, broken and bloodied.

A SPECTATOR (to the uncurious monsieur): Curious play!

THE UNCURIOUS MONSIEUR: You think so, do you?

He shrugs his shoulders, gets up, and leaves.

THE ACTRESS: Ladies and gentlemen, the play that we will have had the honor of presenting for you in an hour or two is entitled "Curiosity Punished."

III

On the sidewalk in front of the curio shop's smashed window, a noseless dwarf sits sobbing.

Slowly the uncurious monsieur comes walking along the pavement and casts a look of disdain at the noseless dwarf.

LE NAIN SANS NEZ (furieux): Je ne demande pas l'aumône, mais ce regard, vous me le paierez!

Il se lève, ramasse un morceau de vitre et se précipitant sur l'incurieux lui tranche la gorge.

L'incurieux s'écroule, le nain se rassoit et, sans nez, rassis, sourit.

THE NOSELESS DWARF (furious): I'm not begging, damn you! But that look of yours... You won't get away with it. I'll make you pay!

He gets up, takes a piece of the broken glass, and, pouncing on the uncurious monsieur, proceeds to slit his throat.

The uncurious monsieur falls in a heap, the dwarf sits down again, calm and composed, and, noseless, smiles.

LA LUNE ET LA NUIT

Cette nuit-là je regardais la lune
Oui j'étais à ma fenêtre
et je la regardais
et puis j'ai quitté ma fenêtre
je me suis déshabillée
je me suis couchée
et puis alors la chambre est devenue très claire
la lune était entrée
Oui j'avais laissé la fenêtre ouverte
et la lune était entrée
Elle était là cette nuit-là dans ma chambre
et elle brillait
J'aurais pu lui parler
J'aurais pu la toucher
Mais je n'ai rien fait
je l'ai seulement regardée
elle paraissait calme et heureuse
j'avais envie de la caresser
mais je ne savais pas comment m'y prendre
Et je restais là... sans bouger
Elle me regardait
elle brillait
elle souriait...
Alors je me suis endormie
et quand je me suis réveillée
c'était déjà le lendemain matin
et... il y avait seulement le soleil
au-dessus des maisons.

THE MOON AND NIGHT

That very night I was looking at the moon
Yes I was at my window
and I was looking at it
and then I left my window
I got undressed
I got into bed
and just then the room became very bright
the moon had come in
Yes I had left the window open
and the moon had come in
There it was in my room that very night
and it was shining
I could have talked to it
I could have touched it
But I didn't do a thing
I just looked at it nothing more
it seemed peaceful and happy
I felt like going and giving it a hug
but I didn't know how to do it
And I stayed there... without moving
It was looking at me
it was shining
it was smiling...
So I went to sleep
and when I woke up
it was morning next day already
and... there was nothing but the sun
up there above the houses.

ROUSSE

Rousse rousse petite lune
un vieux nuage gris te poursuit
mais un bon crayon jaune
écrit son nom soleil sur la porte du jour
et le nuage crève et tu t'enfuis
rousse rousse petite lune
douce petite chose heureuse
plaisir de la nuit

RUSSET

Russet russet little moon
an old gray cloud is chasing you
but a nice yellow pencil-lead will write
its name sun on the door of day
the cloud bursts and you go your way
russet russet little moon
sweet little happy creature you
joy of the night.

ÉLÉPHANT...

Éléphant
je pense souvent à toi
quand je suis tout seul
quand je suis avec les autres
quand je me promène dans la campagne avec une
    petite badine
quand je me lave les dents le matin
et quelquefois quand je dors ton grand corps se
    promène dans mes rêves
Ce n'est pas du respect que j'ai pour toi
je n'ai pas non plus de tendresse comme on dit
je ne suis pas ton ami
je pense à toi comme ça
Je sais que tu existes encore
et je suis content
Tu es le grand animal
je connais tes oreilles
Enfant je suis monté sur toi dans un jardin
je t'ai vu dans les documentaires
je t'ai vu à Hambourg
je t'ai vu en breloque en pain d'épice
je t'ai vu sur la gomme éléphant
Je te vois tel que tu es
Présent comme une véritable chose vivante
Et tout ce que les hommes racontent sur toi
me fait rire
du mauvais rire
Deux points
Que tu te caches pour faire l'amour
que tu te caches pour mourir
Et que les poils de ta queue portent

ELEPHANT...

Elephant
I think of you often
when I'm all alone
when I'm with others
when I'm strolling in the country with a little
    light-hearted lass
when I'm brushing my teeth in the morning
and sometimes when I'm sleeping your big body
    goes strolling through my dreams
It's not because I have respect for you
I don't have tender feelings either as they say
I'm not your friend
I think of you just like that
I know that you still exist
and I'm glad
You're that big beast
I know your ears
As a kid I once climbed up on your back in a zoo
I saw you in documentaries
I saw you in Hamburg
I saw you as a gingerbread charm
I saw you on the big rubber eraser with your name
Now I see you as you are
In the flesh as a real living thing
And everything people say about you
gives me a laugh
a nasty laugh
Colon, to wit:
That you hide when you make love
that you hide when you're going to die
And that the hairs on your tail

bonheur aux amours des humains
Éléphant
Tu es plus beau qu'un nuage
Le nuage pleut quand il crève
mais toi tu te fous des marchands de parapluies
Et quand tu te promènes avec ta femme et tes
      petits dans ton paysage
Tu es plus beau qu'un nuage
Une véritable chose vivante
Tu ne collectionnes pas les timbres-poste
Tu ne portes pas comme l'homme des lunettes
en fausse écaille de tortue
Et quand captif tu passes dans les villes
Tu es indifférent aux choses compliquées
Un homme te pique les fesses pour que tu ailles plus vite
Et tu cours plus vite pour ne pas contrarier le moustique
Si vous arriviez en retard on le foutrait à la porte du cirque
et tu n'y tiens pas—tu cours—
Tu as une drôle de façon de courir
Tu as une drôle de façon de te souvenir

Tu es une véritable chose vivante je ne t'oublie pas
Je pense souvent à toi… je te serre la trompe.

are lucky for human beings in love
Elephant
You're prettier than a cloud
The cloud rains when it bursts
but you don't give a damn for the umbrella-seller
And when you go strolling with your wife and your
    little ones out in the country
You're prettier than a cloud
A real living thing
You don't collect stamps
You don't wear fake tortoise-shell glasses
the way a man does
And when you're roped and paraded through the cities
You couldn't care less about the complicated things
Some man there pricks your butt to make you go faster
And you run faster to keep the mosquito-man happy
If you two got there late they'd kick his ass out of the
    frigging circus
and you wouldn't want that—so you run—
You've got a really funny way of running
You've got a really funny way of remembering

You're a real living thing and I don't forget you
I think of you often… come let me shake your trunk.

LA DERNIÈRE PETITE FEUILLE

La dernière petite feuille d'un arbre
frissonne
dans le vent froid qui lui apporte
les pas du bûcheron

THE LAST LITTLE LEAF

The last little leaf still on the tree
shudders
in the chill wind that brings to her
the woodman's steps approaching.

VILLE D'EAU

Ils se promènent
Ils se rencontrent
Ils se saluent
Ils se font des politesses
Ils échangent des idées
Ils sont laids et abîmés
décorés et honorés
Il y a trop de mauvaise graisse
entre leurs os et leur peau
et l'on dirait que tous les animaux
qu'ils ont mangés
en se laissant manger
se sont vengés
Ils ont trop mangé d'animaux morts
Ils ont pendu par le cou des oiseaux morts et abîmés
Ils ont trop mangé d'oiseaux abîmés
ils ont beaucoup trop bu de vins beaucoup trop vieux
Ils sont trop vieux trop vieux et trop laids
et ils le savent bien
Ils ont mangé et bu la part des autres
et quand ils regardent les autres
ils voudraient bien
les voir crever comme des chiens pauvres
dans un coin
Ils ont le cheveu rare et la mauvaise humeur
Et une façon de regarder sans rien voir
une façon de faire semblant de regarder
semblant de voir
c'est à dégueuler
oui à dégueuler

THE SPA

They stroll
They meet
They greet each other
They proffer their civilities
They offer a few pleasantries
They're ugly and emaciated
honor-lapeled and decorated
There's too much flabby fat between
their bones and skin
as if the beasts that they've done in
the animals their jaws have bested unabated
who've let themselves be chewed digested
take their revenge
They've eaten too much living flesh
hung by the neck dead birds emaciated
eaten too many of those birds emaciated
drunk too much wine too much and much too old
And they're too old too
yes much too old
too ugly and they know it yes they do
They've drunk and eaten other people's share
and when they look on all those folk
they wouldn't care—if truth be told—
if like poor dogs off in a corner there
they'd up and croak
They're sparse of hair they're crochety
And they can make you think it's you who
have caught their eye
while they look through you
repulsively
enough to make you puke

là vraiment
sur-le-champ
Et quand ils boivent leur eau sale
dans des misérables petits gobelets
ils rient d'un atroce petit rire
ils plaisantent en grinçant des dents
et les misères les plus secrètes
de leurs tristes corps condamnés
font très précisément les frais
de leurs confidences obscènes
de leur épouvantable hilarité

ah yes
or puke at less
and suddenly
And when they sip their little swallows
of tacky water from their wretched cups
what follows after is a little fit
of foul and loathsome laughter that commences
with crashing jest and gnashing teeth
and pays for each hacking guffaw as it
racks all their vile and vulgar confidences.

LE STRICT SUPERFLU

Un beau jour
Les hommes qui fabriquent mangeront à leur faim
Et ce qu'ils mangeront sera bon
très bon
pas bon comme la romaine
ou bon pour le service
mais simplement bon
comme le bon pain
Un beau jour
Les hommes qui fabriquent dormiront leur content
et ils auront de beaux rêves
de belles amours
et des draps blancs
et de grandes orgues de Barbarie
qui marcheront au quart de tour
et qui joueront tous les jours
les plus beaux airs du monde
et
les plus difficiles
Parce qu'un jour
les hommes qui fabriquent
connaîtront enfin la musique

THE BARE EXCESS[1]

One day soon
The ones who produce things will eat to their guts' content
And what they eat will be good
very good
not "good as gold" or "good as the day is long"[2]
or "good enough to join the army"
just good
the way good bread is good
One day soon
The ones who produce things will sleep late and linger
in bed if they would
and they'll have nice dreams
nice love affairs too
white sheets
and hurdy-gurdies like organs great and grand
to play
every day
with the flick of a finger the twist of a hand
the world's most delightful
and
demanding music
Because one day soon
the ones who produce things
will finally get the tune

---

[1] Prévert's seemingly Marxist-inspired title, playing on the opposite of *"le strict nécessaire"* (the bare essentials), predicts the reversal of social roles.

[2] I take the liberty of expanding a little on the original's slightly abstruse allusive and elusive clichés.

ÂNE DORMANT

C'est un âne qui dort
Enfants, regardez-le dormir
Ne le réveillez pas
Ne lui faites pas de blagues
Quand il ne dort pas, il est très souvent malheureux.
Il ne mange pas tous les jours.
On oublie de lui donner à boire.
Et puis on tape dessus.
Regardez-le
Il est plus beau que les statues qu'on vous dit d'admirer et qui vous ennuient.
Il est vivant, il respire, confortablement installé dans son rêve.
Les grandes personnes disent que la poule rêve de grain et l'âne d'avoine.
Les grandes personnes disent ça pour dire quelque chose, elles feraient mieux de s'occuper de leurs rêves à elles de leurs petits cauchemars personnels.
Sur l'herbe à côté de sa tête, il y a deux plumes. S'il les a vues avant de s'endormir il rêve peut-être qu'il est oiseau et qu'il vole.
Ou peut-être il rêve d'autre chose.
Par exemple qu'il est à l'école des garçons, caché dans l'armoire aux cartons à dessin.
Il y a un petit garçon qui ne sait pas faire son problème.
Alors le maître lui dit:
Vous êtes un âne, Nicolas!
C'est désastreux pour Nicolas.
Il va pleurer.
Mais l'âne sort de sa cachette
Le maître ne le voit pas.
Et l'âne fait le problème du petit garçon.

SLEEPING ASS

An ass is asleep
Children, look at him sleeping
Don't wake him up
Don't tease him with your pranks
Often, when he's not asleep, he's unhappy.
Some days he doesn't eat.
They forget to give him water.
And they whack him besides.
Look at him
He's prettier than the statues they tell you to admire but that you think are so boring.

He's living and breathing, settled comfortably in his dream.

The grown-ups tell us that hens dream of grain and the ass dreams of oats.

The grown-ups tell us that just to say something.

They'd do better to worry about their personal dreams and their own little nightmares.

Lying on the grass by his head are two feathers. If he saw them before he fell asleep maybe he's dreaming he's a bird and he's flying.

Or maybe he's dreaming something else altogether.

For example that he's at the boys' school hiding in the cupboard where the sketchpads are kept.

And there's this little boy there who can't do his problem.

So the teacher tells him:
Nicolas, you're an ass!
And Nicolas is devastated.
He's about to start crying.
But the ass comes out of hiding.
The teacher doesn't see him.
And the ass does the little boy's problem for him.

Le petit garçon va porter le problème au maître, et le maître dit:
C'est très bien, Nicolas!
Alors l'âne et Nicolas rient tout doucement aux éclats, mais le maître ne les entend pas.
Et si l'âne ne rêve pas ça
C'est qu'il rêve autre chose.
Tout ce qu'on peut savoir, c'est qu'il rêve.
Tout le monde rêve.

The little boy takes the problem up to the teacher and the teacher says:

Very good, Nicolas!

Then Nicolas and the ass break out laughing very softly, but the teacher doesn't hear them.

And if that's not what the ass is dreaming
Then he's dreaming something else.
All we know for sure is that he's dreaming.
Everyone dreams.

ORAGE

Oiseau fou de terreur perdu dans le métro
chagrin multicolère
cauchemar de la mariée
clef de son troupeau de songes aux abattoirs menés
alcôve du secret et caillou dans la mare
météore soudain vert disparu à jamais
ricochet du bonheur étouffé et noyé
sang de la laie mêlé au sang du sanglier
hallali du soleil chassé de la forêt

Mais l'éclair scie l'orage et signe l'éclaircie

Arc en ciel Miró
gentil spectre solaire
dompteur de feux follets

Arc en ciel Miró:

> « L'oiseau s'envole vers la zone
> où le duvet pousse sur les collines
>
> Femmes oiseaux étoiles
>
> Femmes et oiseaux devant la lune »

STORM[1]

Bird mad with terror lost in the underground
polychrome distress
nightmare of the bride
key to the meaning of her flock of dreams led to the slaughter
intimate alcove and pebble in the pond
sudden meteor of green now forever vanished
ricochet of happiness stifled and drowned
blood of the sow and the boar's blood mixed as one
death-blow to the sun hunted out of the forest

But the lightning saws the storm and signs its name
   on the clearing

Rainbow Miró
nice little specter sun
tamer of the will-o'-the-wisps

Rainbow Miró:

      "The bird goes flying toward the zone
       where the hills lie soft with down

         Women birds stars

      Women and birds before the moon"

----

[1] This and the next two poems, inspired by Miró and in keeping with the poet's frequently surrealistic vein, originally appeared, with reproductions, in *Joan Miró* (1956), by Prévert and G. Ribemont-Dessaignes.

OASIS MIRÓ

Des oiseaux jaune fou vêtus de noir brûlé
dans un ciel noir désert
volaient

Vert Vert
Garcia Lorca chantait
Astre de cuivre rouge son cœur les attirait

Est-ce la faute de la lune
les larmes sont salées
et les plus fines lames de la mer
viennent se briser comme verre
sur le plus tendre des rochers

les larmes sont salées
est-ce la faute de la lune
qui régit les marées.

MIRÓ OASIS

Birds of wild yellow dressed in a burnt black
in a black empty sky
would fly

Green Green[1]
García Lorca singing
Red copper star his heart calling them back

Is moon at fault
tears taste of salt
the ocean's finest breakers thrashing flinging
themselves ashore and smashing
against the tenderest cliff like glass

tears taste of salt
is moon at fault
moon the tides' master.

---

[1] The reference is to the opening and recurring line in García Lorca's celebrated "Romance sonámbulo," "Verde que te quiero verde," in his *Romancero gitano* (1928).

MIROIR MIRÓ

Il y a un miroir dans le nom de Miró
parfois dans ce miroir un univers de vignes de raisins et de vin

Tache solaire
jaune d'œuf précolombien
l'oiseau tonnerre roucoule dans le lointain

Ivre déjà depuis midi
entraînant avec lui la nappe du matin
le soleil noir s'écroule dans la cave du soir

Pénombre grise et ombre déportée
rouge fracas du vert brisé

La blanchisseuse veuve qu'on appelle la nuit
surgit sans bruit
et dans le bleu de sa lessive
l'astre à Miró
l'étoile tardive
luit...

MIRROR MIRÓ

There is a mirror in the name Miró
at times in that mirror a universe of vines and grapes and wine

Sunspot
egg yolk from pre-Columbian days
and in the distance cooing the thunder bird

Drunk now since noon
and dragging off the morning coverlet
black sun collapsing into evening's cave

Penumbra gray and shade displaced
red fracas of the fractured green

The widow washerwoman that they call night
looms noiselessly
and in her spreading wash of blue
Miró's orb
tardy star
shines through...

JE M'ENDORS...

Je m'endors avec des oiseaux plein les yeux
Et je rêve d'un jardin
Mais si tes yeux sont loin des miens
Je m'endors avec des larmes plein les yeux
Et mon rêve s'appelle: chagrin.

I FALL ASLEEP...

I fall asleep birds fill my eyes
I dream of garden loveliness
Far from your eyes contrariwise
I fall asleep tears fill my eyes
And my dream bears the name: distress.

AU DEMEURANT...

À Georges Malkine

Dans la demeure de la liberté tout s'était très bien passé,
le futur était arrivé.

Soudain, de la bouche d'un témoin, sortirent quatre vérités:
le futur avait un passé.

Dans la demeure de la fiancée, c'est encore hier et déjà demain,
mais le futur loin.

Vide est la corbeille, fermées les portes, tirés les rideaux.

Il n'y a pas de présent, le temps ne fait pas de cadeaux.

AFTER ALL...

For Georges Malkine[1]

In freedom's dwelling all had gone well, the future groom had arrived.

Suddenly, from the lips of a witness, the simple truth came out: the future groom had a past.

In the bride's dwelling, it's yesterday still and tomorrow already, but far off is the future groom.

The gifts are gone, the doors closed shut, and the curtains are drawn.

There is no present, time doesn't give gifts.

---

[1] Georges Malkine (1898–1970) was a noted surrealist painter and filmmaker, friend of Breton and many other celebrities of the movement, Prévert among them.

LE CŒUR CHERCHEUR

C'est les grandes manœuvres
Un caporal d'ordinaire commande les ordinateurs.
Ailleurs
des déserteurs avec des moyens de fortune bricolent des extraordi-
    nateurs sauvages d'une apparente simplicité enfantine mais
    d'une merveilleuse et redoutable efficacité mondiale.

THE SEARCHING HEART[1]

It's army maneuvers time
A non-com(putant) mess corporal mans the computers
Elsewhere
deserters with salvaged bits and pieces improvise primitive com-
   pudigious machines of an apparently infantile simplicity but
   of a wondrous and fearsome efficiency the wide world over.

---

[1] I translate the title literally, though with no clear suggestion as to what the poet
would have it mean. It does not seem related to either of the succeeding puns,
"caporal d'ordinaire" and *"extraordinateurs,"* both playing—none too subtly—on
"ordinateur."

RÊVE

Nous sommes sur un bateau, très nombreux mais debout.
Serrés, les uns contre les autres, bien plus serrés encore que
dans le Métro, aux « heures de pointe ».
Une voix réclame une cabine, une autre parle du prochain
port.
Aucune réponse.
Une voix encore, inquiète, angoissée:
« et le mal de mer alors! »
Alors c'est le tangage, le roulis et puis...
et puis je me réveille avant que le rêve ne devienne,
peut-être, écœurant cauchemar.

(Lundi 10 juin 1974)

DREAM

We're all on a boat, a crowd but all standing.
Pressed against one another, even worse than at
"rush hours" in the Métro.
A voice yells for a cabin, another one talks about
getting into port.
No answer.
Another voice, harried and distraught:
"And talk about seasick!"
Then the pitching, the tossing, the rolling, and then...
and then I wake up before the dream, *perhaps,* can
turn into a gut-wrenching nightmare.

(Monday 10 June 1974)

ADAGE

Sur une plage déserte
une tortue à l'envers
auprès d'un sablier
Personne pour les retourner

Tortue
ta dernière heure
ne sera point comptée.

ADAGE

On a deserted beach
a turtle lying on her ass
beside an hourglass
And no one to turn over each

Turtle
your dying hour will pass
uncounted.

COMPLAINTE DE LA MER...

Complainte de la mer
          dans le fracas du vent
Tout ce qu'elle vocifère
et qu'elle chante en rêvant
dans les sables mouvants
Tout ce qu'elle tait soudain
Silencieuse
étale
et plate calmement

LAMENT OF THE OCEAN...

Lament of the ocean
       roaring tempest-fanned
All that commotion
that sing-song chanting
over the shifting sand
sung in its dreams
Then all that sudden quiet that
silence that seems
so calm
so stagnant
flat.

HAGIOGRAPHIE ET ICONOGRAPHIE

En examinant même rapidement les images saintes, les illustrations et bibles, de catéchismes et autres livres édifiants et sacrés, on constate que les animaux créés par Dieu avant l'homme nous apparaissent comme nos contemporains tout aussi bien que ceux d'Adam.

Et, diluviens ou antédiluviens, les agneaux, les oiseaux, les tigres, les éléphants, le serpent d'Ève, la baleine de Jonas ou la colombe de Noé sont les semblables des bêtes de nos jours.

Cela nous porte à croire que la terre, à une très incertaine époque, a été dédinosaurisée.

Dieu défait vite et bien ce qu'il fait.

HAGIOGRAPHY AND ICONOGRAPHY

When we examine even quickly the sacred images, the biblical illustrations, in catechisms and other holy and edifying books, we notice that the animals created by God before the appearance of Man seem to be like the ones with whom we live quite as much as do Adam's.

And, whether diluvian or antediluvian, the lambs, birds, tigers, elephants, Eve's serpent, Jonah's whale, or Noah's dove are the equals of the beasts that we know in our own day.

Which leads us to believe that the earth, at a most indeterminate epoch in the past, was dedinosaurized.

God unmakes quickly and well what he makes.

JOURS DE SORTIE

Le père et mère d'Ève s'appelait Adam
Un jour Ève qui sortait des flancs d'Adam
rencontra Dionysos qui sortait de la cuisse de Jupiter
et laissa tomber Adam
Et Adam resta tout seul avec sa petite famille,
garçons et filles qui vécurent malheureux
et qui eurent beaucoup d'enfants.

DAYS OUT

The father and mother of Eve was named Adam
One day Eve who came out of Adam's flank
meets Dionysos, out of Jupiter's thigh
and leaves Adam high and dry
Alone with his little family was Adam
boys and girls who had lots of kids too
unhappy that they had 'em.

LA MÉNINGERIE

Dressage,
Dompteurs
de cœurs
et de cerveaux,
pollueurs
de la plus belle eau
du plus bel âge,
ils font sauter dans leurs cerceaux
les enfants sauvages

BRAINTRAINED

Trainers
who train
youth's heart
youth's brain
first-water polluters[1]
of life's fairest age
who teach their loop-the-loops
and who
make children still unspoiled jump through
their hoops

---

[1] The expression *"de la plus belle"* or *"de la première eau"* (of the finest [or first]
water) is a jeweler's term referring to a gem's brilliance. Prévert's wordplay, which
I try to suggest, adds polluted waters to the mix.

L'ENFANCE...

L'enfance
dans le lointain de la jeunesse
l'adolescent la méprise et ne veut pas l'entendre
ce n'est plus moi dit-il
c'est un petit qui ne sait pas ce qu'il dit
mais le petit dit ce qu'il sait
même et surtout quand il se tait
    L'adolescent grandit
il n'a pas étouffé tous les cris
Il n'a effacé ni les
rires ni les larmes...
    Les éducateurs
veulent le jeter dans le grand pareil au même
il ne veut pas penser au pas
il ne veut pas rêver à la baguette...

il veut l'enfance.

CHILDHOOD...

Childhood
from youth's far-distant point
the adolescent scorns it wants no part of it
that's not me now he says
that's a baby who doesn't know
what he's talking about
but the baby is talking about what he knows
even most of all when he doesn't say a thing
   The adolescent grows
he hasn't choked off every cry and shout
He hasn't rubbed out
the laughs or the tears...
   The educators
would cast him into the great all-the-same
he doesn't want to think in step
he doesn't want to dream by the numbers...

what he wants is childhood.

RECORDS DU MONDE

Guerre de Cent Ans.
Guerre de Trente ans.
Guerre de Sept ans.
De quatre ans.
De cinq ans…

Guerre d'une demi-minute gagnée au cent millième de seconde.

WORLD RECORDS

Hundred Years' War
Thirty Years' War
Seven Years' War
Four years.
Five years...

Half-minute war won in a hundred-thousandth of a second.

FOLKLORE

J'ai vu dans les landes, perchés sur de très hautes échasses, des gaveurs d'oies géantes.

Non loin de là, des massacreurs de tourterelles tendaient leurs filets entre les arbres pour piéger les palombes de la paix.

Un peu plus loin encore, dans une clairière un homme tirait. D'autres l'applaudissaient et le proclamaient grand chasseur devant l'Éternel.

Mais derrière l'Éternel un écureuil se foutait de sa gueule.

FOLKLORE

I saw over the moors, perched on very tall stilts, force-feeders of giant geese.

Not far beyond, turtle-doves' assassins were spreading their nets between the trees to trap the doves of peace.

A little farther still, off in a clearing, a man was taking shots. Others were applauding and proclaimed him the master hunter before the Eternal.

But behind the Eternal's back a squirrel thumbed his nose and thought "go screw!"[1]

---

[1] It's not clear from the original *"se foutait de sa gueule"* just whom the irreverent squirrel was mocking, the hunter or the Eternal. Let the reader decide.

Je suis foutu! je ne peux plus lire, ni écrire!
je suis un autre!
Un autre qui regarde celui d'avant,
sans intérêt d'ailleurs.

Une nuit de mars 1977

I'm screwed! I can't read anymore, I can't write!
I'm someone else!
Someone who looks at the one before
and couldn't care less.

A night in March 1977[1]

---

[1] Prévert died on April 11, 1977.

ABOUT THE TRANSLATOR

NORMAN R. SHAPIRO, honored as one of the leading contemporary translators of French, holds the B.A., M.A., and Ph.D. from Harvard University and, as Fulbright scholar, the *Diplôme de Langue et Lettres Françaises* from the Université d'Aix-Marseille. He is Professor of Romance Languages and Literatures at Wesleyan University and is currently Writer in Residence at Adams House, Harvard University. His many published volumes span the centuries, medieval to modern, and the genres: poetry, novel, and theater. Among them are *Four Farces by Georges Feydeau; The Comedy of Eros: Medieval French Guides to the Art of Love; Selected Poems from Baudelaire's 'Les Fleurs du Mal'; One Hundred and One Poems of Paul Verlaine* (recipient of the Modern Language Association's [MLA] Scaglione Award); *Negritude: Black Poetry from Africa and the Caribbean;* and *Creole Echoes: The Francophone Poetry of Nineteenth-Century Louisiana.*

A specialist in French fable literature, Shapiro has also published *Fables from Old French: Aesop's Beasts and Bumpkins* and *The Fabulists French: Verse Fables of Nine Centuries.* His translations of La Fontaine are considered by many to be the definitive voicing into English of this famed French poet. His critically acclaimed volumes include *Fifty Fables of La Fontaine; Fifty More Fables of La Fontaine; Once Again, La Fontaine;* and his recent *The Complete Fables of Jean de La Fontaine* for which he was awarded the MLA's prestigious Lewis Galantiere Prize.

His recent title, *French Women Poets of Nine Centuries: The Distaff and the Pen,* won the 2009 National Translation Award from the American Literary Translators Association. It also won two 2008 PROSE Awards from the Association of American Publishers, for the Best Single-Volume Reference in the Humanities and Social Sciences and for Excellence in Reference Works.

Other new titles include a completely reset and reillustrated version of *La Fontaine's Bawdy: Of Libertines, Louts, and Lechers;* and *To Speak, to Tell You? Poems by Sabine Sicaud.* A comprehensive anthology of poems by Anna de Noailles—*A Life of Poems, Poems of a Life*—will be published soon. Shapiro is a member of the Academy of American Poets.

TITLES FROM BLACK WIDOW PRESS

TRANSLATION SERIES

A Life of Poems, Poems of a Life
by Anna de Noailles. Translated by Norman
R. Shapiro. Introduction by Catherine Perry.

Approximate Man and Other Writings
by Tristan Tzara. Translated and edited by
Mary Ann Caws.

Art Poétique
by Guillevic. Translated by Maureen Smith.

The Big Game
by Benjamin Péret. Translated with an
introduction by Marilyn Kallet.

Capital of Pain
by Paul Éluard. Translated by Mary Ann
Caws, Patricia Terry, and Nancy Kline.

Chanson Dada: Selected Poems
by Tristan Tzara. Translated with an
introduction and essay by Lee Harwood.

Essential Poems and Writings of Joyce Mansour:
A Bilingual Anthology
Translated with an introduction by
Serge Gavronsky.

Essential Poems and Prose of Jules Laforgue
Translated and edited by Patricia Terry.

Essential Poems and Writings of Robert Desnos:
A Bilingual Anthology
Edited with an introduction and essay by
Mary Ann Caws.

EyeSeas (Les Ziaux) by Raymond Queneau.
Translated with an introduction by Daniela
Hurezanu and Stephen Kessler.

Furor and Mystery & Other Writings
by René Char. Edited and translated by
Mary Ann Caws and Nancy Kline.

The Inventor of Love & Other Writings
by Gherasim Luca. Translated by Julian &
Laura Semilian. Introduction by Andrei
Codrescu. Essay by Petre Răileanu.

La Fontaine's Bawdy
by Jean de La Fontaine. Translated with an
introduction by Norman R. Shapiro.

Last Love Poems of Paul Eluard
Translated with an introduction by
Marilyn Kallet.

Love, Poetry (L'amour la poésie) by Paul Eluard.
Translated with an essay by Stuart Kendall.

Poems of André Breton: A Bilingual Anthology
Translated with essays by Jean-Pierre Cauvin
and Mary Ann Caws.

Poems of A. O. Barnabooth by Valéry Larbaud.
Translated by Ron Padgett and Bill Zavatsky.

Poems of Consummation by Vicente Aleixandre.
Translated by Stephen Kessler

Préversities: A Jacques Prévert Sampler
Translated and edited by Norman R. Shapiro.

The Sea and Other Poems
by Guillevic. Translated by Patricia Terry.
Introduction by Monique Chefdor.

To Speak, to Tell You? Poems by Sabine Sicaud.
Translated by Norman R. Shapiro. Intro-
duction and notes by Odile Ayral-Clause.

forthcoming translations

Guarding the Air:
Selected Poems of Gunnar Harding
Translated and edited by Roger Greenwald.

Pierre Reverdy: Poems Early to Late
Translated by Mary Ann Caws and
Patricia Terry.

Jules Supervielle: Selected Poems
Translated by Nancy Kline and Patricia Terry.

Boris Vian Invents Boris Vian:
A Boris Vian Reader
Edited and translated by Julia Older.

MODERN POETRY SERIES

ABC of Translation by Willis Barnstone

An Alchemist with One Eye on Fire
by Clayton Eshleman

Anticline by Clayton Eshleman

Archaic Design by Clayton Eshleman

Backscatter: New and Selected Poems
by John Olson

The Caveat Onus by Dave Brinks

City Without People: The Katrina Poems
by Niyi Osundare

Concealments and Caprichos
by Jerome Rothenberg

Crusader-Woman
by Ruxandra Cesereanu. Translated by Adam
J. Sorkin. Introduction by Andrei Codrescu.

Curdled Skulls: Poems of Bernard Bador
Translated by the author with
Clayton Eshleman.

Endure: Poems by Bei Dao. Translated by
Clayton Eshleman and Lucas Klein.

Exile is My Trade: A Habib Tengour Reader
Translated by Pierre Joris.

Fire Exit by Robert Kelly

Forgiven Submarine by Ruxandra Cesereanu
and Andrei Codrescu

from stone this running by Heller Levinson

The Grindstone of Rapport:
A Clayton Eshleman Reader

Larynx Galaxy by John Olson

The Love That Moves Me
by Marilyn Kallet

Memory Wing by Bill Lavender

Packing Light: New and Selected Poems
by Marilyn Kallet

The Present Tense of the World:
Poems 2000–2009 by Amina Saïd. Translated
with an introduction by Marilyn Hacker.

The Price of Experience by Clayton Eshleman

The Secret Brain: Selected Poems 1995–2012
by Dave Brinks

Signal from Draco: New and Selected Poems
by Mebane Robertson

forthcoming modern poetry titles

An American Unconscious
by Mebane Robertson

Eye of Witness: A Jerome Rothenberg Reader
Edited with commentaries by
Heriberto Yepez & Jerome Rothenberg

Memory by Bernadette Mayer

LITERARY THEORY /
BIOGRAPHY SERIES

Revolution of the Mind:
The Life of André Breton
by Mark Polizzotti

Clayton Eshleman: The Whole Art
Edited by Stuart Kendall. (forthcoming)

LOUISIANA HERITAGE SERIES
Second Line Press imprint

Jules Choppin: New Orleans Poems
in Creole and French
Translated by Norman R. Shapiro.
Introduction by M. Lynn Weiss.

Dinner at Antoine's (forthcoming)
by Francis Parkinson Keyes

Crescent Carnival (forthcoming)
by Francis Parkinson Keyes

WWW.BLACKWIDOWPRESS.COM

This book was set in Adobe Caslon,
a typeface designed by Carol Twombly
as a variation on Caslon's specimen pages
printed between 1734 and 1770.
The titling font is Kolo, which was
inspired by the lettering of Koloman
Moser, Gustav Klimt, and Alfred Roller.